ALL RISE!

THE SICKLE CELL COMMUNITY

VS.

THE MEDICAL ESTABLISHMENT.

To: Aniekan Uwan,
My amazing husband who calls me "beautiful" even as he cares for my ailing body.
May God grant your desires for the decent human being that you are.
Thank you for being my earthly constant.

Table of Contents

Acknowledgements

Acknowledgments to Physicians and Nurses known for your care, penned by some of your patients: You have tenderly cared for Sickle Cell patients. Thank you for all that you have done and continue to do for the Sickle Cell community. You have fought for us, cared for us, and loved us. You will never truly know what that means to us! May abundant blessings be yours for this kindness.

Dr. Elliott S. Wolfe, former Associate Dean of Student Affairs, Stanford University School of Medicine. - Thank you for your solid and consistent help as I navigated through medical school with Sickle Cell disease. Endless gratitude for you!!!

Dr. John Faul, Dept of Pulmonology, Stanford University Hospital. - Thank you for your detailed care that picked up what others missed. Grateful for you!

Dr. Lawrence Leung, Stanford University Hospital Dept. of Hematology. - For your constant hand in managing my care. For listening to me. For being the ONLY doctor to consider me deserving of an apology after being under-treated by a resident.

Dr. Pierre Fotso, ORMC, Orlando, FL. - Your attention to detail and humanity was obvious from the first time you took care of me. My family loves you. Never stop being excellent!

Dr. Beth Martin, Stanford University Hospital. - Thank you for being ahead of you time, for your care and for helping to make sure your colleagues cared for me in your absence.

ALL RISE!

Dr. Lanetta Bronté-Hall. - Foundation for Sickle Cell Disease Research and Education. Thank you for your tireless efforts on behalf of the Sickle Cell community and for treating us like family!

Dr. Marsha Treadwell, UCSF Benioff Children's Hospital. - You are making a tremendous difference in countless lives! Your compassion is so obvious!!! WE SEE YOU!!!

Dr. Keith Quirolo, Children's Hospital Oakland, CA. - Magic! Infinite heartfelt praise and thanks for all your teaching to the community and all your work behind the scenes. Amazing tireless work! WE SEE YOU!!!

Dr. Oya Tugal, Pediatric Hematology/Oncology at Maria Fareri Children's Hospital, Westchester Medical. - "You have gone above and beyond for my daughters"

Jennifer Valentin, RN. Emergency Department, Oviedo Medical Center, FL. - My infusion nurse who is so passionate and human. Became my friend and still is. Making an amazing difference in countless lives.

Dr. Robert Molokie UIC, Chicago. - Thank you!

Dr. Sharon Jackson, Medical Univ. of South Carolina. - Thank you!

Dr. Ify Osunkwo, Atrium Medical Center/Levine Cancer and Oncology Center Charlotte NC. - 1) "She is one of the best specialists in Sickle Cell in the entire country."

   And...

2) "Always showed genuine care and went beyond the call for my family for almost two decades."

Dr. Margaret Oloo of St. Luke medical centre in Kisumu, Kenya. - Thank You!

Dr. Boateng of Koforidua Central Hospital. Ghana. - Thank You!

Dr. Murtala Muhd. Kano State, Nigeria. - Thank You!

Dr. Wanda Shurney in Detroit. - "She is an angel and lifesaver in this community. Thank You!"

Professor Essien, Dr. Mabel Ekanem, Dr. Timothy Ekwere, Dr. Idongesit Akpan, all in University of Uyo Teaching Hospital, Nigeria. - Thank You!

Rosemary Britts, Executive Director of Sickle Cell Assoc.- "Does MUCH for Sickle Cell with so little. Sickle Cell Association in Missouri (Florissant). Barnes Jewish Hospital. Thank You!"

Dr. Cage Johnson, LA County/USC Medical Center. -Thank You!

Dr. Morey Blinder at Washington Univ. Physicians. - Thank You!

Dr. Mary Henehan, Dr. James D'Olimpio, Dr. Ilean Friedman. -Thank You!

Nurse Irene Fisher, Nurse Ethan Greenwood, MS. - Thank You!

ALL RISE!

Dr. Douglas Collins at Metro Hematology/Oncology Center in Atlanta, GA. - Just for going above and beyond all the time for his patients. Thank you

Dr. Peroutka, Andrews and Patel Assoc. Camp Hill, PA. - Thank You!

Dr. Patricia Graves, Memphis TN. - Thank You!

Dr Fortune. Hannel Clinic Trans Ekulu, Enugu, Nigeria. - He has been so wonderful to me. Thank You!

Dr. Alan Anderson, Comprehensive Sickle Cell Program, Greenville, SC. - Thank You!

Dr. Ramamoorthy Nagasubramanian, MD Pediatric Hematology-Oncology Nemours. - Thank You!

Pat Corley, RN. - Thank You!

Dr. Alex at Phoenix Children's Hospital on the Bone Marrow transplant team in Phoenix AZ. - Thank You!

Brook at Phoenix Children's hospital in Phoenix Arizona. - Thank You!

Nurses Vera Lewis, Jessie Thomas (retired). - Thank You!

Dr. Ajazz and **Nurse Chelly, Avant Celebration Hospital.** - "They take really good care of me with my appointments and my hospitalizations. Thanks!"

ALL RISE!

Catherine Bock Burns RN. - "She is truly a blessing. My fighter when I'm too weak to fight. My angel and my 2nd mom. Thanks!"

Dr. Maria Regina Flores Florida Cancer Specialists. Orlando Florida. - Thank You!

Dr. Stephen Kronish, Kaiser Hospital Oakland, CA. - Thank You!

Dr. Curtis Owens, Methodist Comprehensive Sickle Cell Clinic; Memphis, TN. - Thank You!

Dr. Stephen C. Nelson. Children's Minnesota. - Thank You!
And countless others whose patients never saw this request for your names...

ALL RISE!

"A powerful message from the Sickle Cell patients' community to healthcare providers. This book turns the spotlight on the prejudice they face when seeking care."

~ *Pierre Fotso MD*
Assoc. Director of Inpatient Medicine, Orlando Regional Medical Center, FL.

"Thought provoking and informative. It does not sugar coat medical provider's very real lackadaisical approach in pain management in as misunderstood a community as Sickle Cell patients. It's a bird's eye view into a patient's experience from a doctor with Sickle Cell disease. It forces a hard look into our own practices and obstacles in providing efficient, SAFE care."

~ *Jennifer Valentin, RN*
Emergency Department, Oviedo Medical Center

"The book All Rise provides great amounts of insights into the journey of life faced by many warriors fighting Sickle Cell enduring challenges with a concerning healthcare approach that lacks quality and supportive care. Dr. Simone Uwan presents a need for change to understand the best approach for the healthcare community to provide quality care needed for Sickle Cell warriors to survive and thrive the fight for their life! This book and its analytical approach has inspired me as a mother of a Sickle Cell warrior and international advocate, and I would recommend the book to all healthcare students, providers and communities with interest."

~ *Carla Lewis*
CEO and Founder of "Kids Conquering Sickle Cell Disease Foundation Inc.", Co-Founder of the Young Adult Sickle Cell Alliance, National Sickle Cell Research Advocate & Facilitator.

"For far too long, the Sickle Cell community has been ignored, but *All Rise!* is the best explanation I have seen for the normal people and healthcare practitioners to understand what Sickle Cell is.

Dr. Uwan identifies the problems and recommends best solutions to solve these issues. *All Rise!* is a must-read whether you have Sickle Cell, are in the medical field or just concerned. I recommend this book wholeheartedly!"
~*Ethleen Peacock*

Sickle Cell warrior, Founder of Alaafia Women and Strength in Sickle Cell support groups.

"Simone Uwan, MD has captured the voices of many with Sickle Cell who must interact with the medical community on a regular basis. This book should be required reading for any medical provider caring for those with Sickle Cell disease."
~*Allan F. Platt PA-C, MMSc, DFAAPA*

Assistant Professor, Director of Admissions Physician Assistant Program, Emory University School of Medicine, co-author of the book "Hope and Destiny" for Sickle Cell disease management.

"Simone's book is perfect! Her medical expertise just shines through. If only they could clone her! This book is such an important book. It should be on the list of required reading for the doctors and nurses.

I could not have written this book. I don't have the vocabulary to tell the story this way. But she does! And I can't say enough about it."

~Judy Gray Johnson

A thriver with Sickle Cell disease, Educator, prolific international author of "Living with Sickle Cell Disease", "The Struggle to Survive", and "Resilience: Coping with Sickle Cell Disease".

INTRODUCTION

I come before you as a once reluctant Sickle Cell advocate, wet behind the ears. Looking back, I really deserve a spanking from the universe for the number of excuses I made and the amount of time that has been wasted as a result. Nowadays, when I attend any Sickle Cell event, the natural and awkward question has been, "Where have *you* been?"

That is a good question. Where *have* I been? A doctor and a patient who could bridge the gap between the two worlds hiding away and finally appearing on the advocacy scene in her late 40's (I boast about my age by the way. It means I'm not dead)? My only answer has been that just like the year has seasons, so do people. I have been able to accomplish many things in my life as a "foreigner" who came to the United States as a child. I have been able to work with and learn from some of the most amazing people researching Thalassemia and Sickle Cell disease. I completed medical school and residency and had the joy of treating patients with Sickle Cell the way they deserved, with their self-esteem not only intact but bettered.

I practiced medicine and juggled that life of doctor and patient for several years and enjoyed bringing back compassionate, yet competent, medicine to whoever needed it. I was never far away from the happenings of the Sickle Cell community, finding ways to make life a little easier for those who asked my help. I advocated for any Sickle Cell patient who called me in the throes of a bad Sickle Cell crisis(flare) to stand in as their medical doctor and speak to anyone on their care team.

But I always stayed under the radar. I believed the lie that I was ordinary and that many others had my dual designation of doctor and patient. They would likely have more energy than me to do the job of advocacy between the healthcare industry and the Sickle Cell Community.

However, many of my "seasons" were filled with unreasonable physical pain and kept me too busy to think past my own care and wellbeing at times. Finally, after years of documenting my journey, I received that spiritual tap on the shoulder to lift my head and share my journey because others needed it. So, I did. I wrote a book called "A Doctor In a Patient's Body; Dreaming Big with Sickle Cell Disease and Chronic Pain" and it became an Amazon #1 Bestseller.

I would never have anticipated such a warm, global response! It has been overwhelming at times but glorious. However, it seems like wherever I look, the need is overwhelming, and the pleas for help comes from everywhere. It became obvious that I had to do something. It was not an option.

With this book, I am attempting to bridge that gap between the healthcare community and my people suffering from this ailment often too difficult to carry. I urge each side to appreciate the challenges of the other. But the balance of power is quite unequal. I hope I can accomplish this task.

I was told not to "talk down" to you. But I also do not want to talk up to you just to flaunt medical language and shroud vital information in the process. After all, I am not trying to hide this information from the rest of the world as I share it with you. So, whenever it comes up, and it is appropriate, medical terminology or medicalese is what I will use. Otherwise, likely for some of you, for the first time in Sickle Cell disease, you will be hearing not just from a patient, but from a colleague as well. This time the Sickle Cell patient is the medical doctor-me!

When was the last time you listened sincerely to any of your patients with the intent of learning whatever you could from the conversation? When have you ever treated your patient as an expert? You are busy learning many things. But I can almost promise you that some of what I have to say, you have rarely, if ever, heard. That is because regardless of how compassionate the doctors studying Sickle Cell disease are, they do not "live in the house."

I "live in the house" of Sickle Cell disease and have had to learn the structure and function of that house to survive. Thanks to my medical education from Columbia University and Stanford School of Medicine, I also have the medical understanding and terminology in which to frame my experience of this house. Those who study Sickle Cell have had to peek through the windows and around the doors, and this limits their findings and understanding. I want nothing more than to bridge that gap.

You can do an online search and likely find 150,000 entries on asthma. If you are lucky, you will find 10,000 entries about Sickle Cell disease. For us patients, much of what our 'house' looks like, only we know. People are dying needlessly because there is a lack of knowledge among healthcare providers, meshed often with an arrogance that makes the task of educating those in healthcare daunting for a patient. However, if the provider does not have adequate information to treat us, who does?

The Canadian physician and one of the four founding professors of Johns Hopkins Hospital, Sir William Osler, once said, "A physician who treats himself has a fool for a patient." I first saw that quote on the office wall of a Dean at one of the universities I attended. Initially, this caused me great consternation, but in time I have realized that this quote is inaccurate. It sounds beautiful, very smart even, but it is flawed.

The concern that the doctor would treat herself as a patient rests on the presumption that there are others more capable of treating the patient. In time I have come to see that this is not always the case. Every century is filled with failed medical theories, hypotheses that were not substantiated when tested. Conversely, there have been pioneers who had to do a lonely walk of discovery, that might have even been laughed at until the rest of the world caught on.

Sometimes there was little support for my hypotheses because I was likely regarded as just a young medical student saddled with a debilitating disease. But, when time is of the essence, and your life is on the line, you can't afford to wait until the rest of the medical establishment decides to expand their knowledge of your disease. You do those experiments yourself, with your limited experimental group, that n of 1! And sometimes, you might even convince a group of friends with the same disorder to test your hypotheses along with you, creating your own study. I was that lowly medical student. I learned quite a bit, and thankfully what started out as "n=1 grew steadily to eventually become N=300 from a pool of 20,000 Sickle Cell warriors from all across the globe." Pretty cool, if you ask me.

Please remember as you read that I am speaking to a vast audience in healthcare, from medical doctors who have no clue about Sickle Cell disease or its management, to the nursing establishment and their students who are at various stages of learning. I am also speaking to medical students who are likely in different years of learning in school, and so they will be in a similar boat. I want everyone to learn, and as such, I will need to address every issue at the least common denominator. Please do not take offense. I am not trying to insult your intelligence, but I am simply making room at the table for everyone who wants to learn.

ALL RISE!

Part 1

CHAPTER ONE

EXCITING TIMES!

These are exciting times in the world of Sickle Cell Disease, and it can almost seem like it has always been so. The American Society of Hematology (ASH) is admitting that not enough has been done for the advancement and treatment of Sickle Cell disease.[1] This year 2019, they formed a task force-ASH Research Collaborative[2] and they traveled to states with high Sickle Cell demographics (mine included) to meet and talk with us, the Sickle Cell community (I was there) and to let us know they saw that we had not been fairly represented in treatments for our disease and wanted to make up for this.

They acknowledged that more had been accomplished for Cystic Fibrosis, another rare disease with similar incidence, than for Sickle Cell disease.[3] Wanting to make up for this discrepancy, they asked our input on how best to meet our medical needs, and what we as Sickle Cell patients believe could be done to create more treatments for patients not eligible for stem cell transplant. We talked about the possibility of a cure and how to make that available to everyone.

THANK YOU, ASH. Truth and reconciliation!

I see the FDA finally correcting themselves about where we, the Sickle Cell community, stand in the opioid epidemic. They are now making sure to tell folks that indeed we are not drug-seeking, but that these heavy-hitting medicines were designed for such a time as the life-threatening and enormously painful Sickle Cell crisis that occurs so often in Sickle Cell disease. They have now corrected the guidelines to exclude us, along with cancer patients and people having surgery, from the tight restrictions generated in response to the massive uptick in opioid abuse.[4] And there are experts in the field who, having done their retrospective analysis, verified that while there was an increase in opioid abuse in the general population, there was no significant increase in opioid use in the Sickle Cell community![5,6] Imagine that!

I read an article where the head of Pediatric Hematology at Harvard said that indeed, a Sickle Cell crisis is like a heart attack. [7] Funny, I had done a video on this exact topic two months prior, likening a Sickle Cell crisis to a heart attack. I argued my point and posted the video all over Facebook. I arrived at this conclusion based on common sense and human pathophysiology. But it sounds better, even more profound when it comes from this medical doctor who is the head of a Hematology department at Harvard University.

And not just him! Although that would have been good enough, the cosmos saw it fit to add a second voice on the heels of the first, this time from a cancer research doctor. He explained how they used Sickled Cells, because of their tendency to clog vessels and cause bone and tissue infarcts, to kill off cancer cells by blocking the vessels leading to it.[8] See? I knew our cells could be good for something!

As I shared in my first book, it was this musing train of thought of what disease my cells might cure that was profaned once during my blood exchange transfusion. I watched a nurse nonchalantly toss the bag of my red blood cells into a trash can marked "hazardous waste." Likely at the very same time, at another research institution, someone had the good sense to make use of these red blood cells. It's sad that those red blood cells treat our good tissue like it treats cancer, clogging our vessels that lead to.... well... everything![9] But kudos for cancer research, sincerely.

Lastly, an idea has been developed that has the potential to greatly minimize the madness when it comes to lack of standardization of care in Sickle Cell disease. This can happen as you move not just from one state to another, but from one doctor to another within any given hospital system! The proposed solution uses a telemedicine and tele-mentoring system called Project ECHO, created by the University of New Mexico, and which has been in existence for over a decade.[10] This model can be used for any type of medicine.

In this case, it is being used for the management of Sickle Cell disease. Project ECHO for Sickle Cell has several hubs around the country. A panel of medical experts in the treatment of Sickle Cell disease is available to assist any healthcare provider in the community by giving expert feedback as these providers navigate the sometimes murky waters of managing Sickle Cell disease.[11] What an opportunity to manage patients uniformly as much as that is possible, and still provide individualized care with each call!

There is also a hub located at Virginia Commonwealth University (Virginia Sickle Cell Disease ECHO), and very recently, I was invited to be on the panel as a contributor from a patient perspective. I am excited to be able to see how things work. My heart's desire is to see these Sickle Cell ECHO projects, wherever they are, grow wings and fly.

It might appear that we are not doing too badly, at least not right now. There is also great news of novel treatments on the horizon for us with Sickle Cell disease! I would not be surprised if we found a low-cost cure available to everyone across the globe in my lifetime. What a present that would be for the truly devastating disease that Sickle Cell is.

Seriously, take a look at the rollout of goodies we either now have, or will be working with. In fact, let us chat a little about each treatment we currently know for Sickle Cell disease.

References

1. ASH Sickle Cell Disease Summit: A Call to Action. ASH Clinical News, MAY 1, 2015 https://www.ashclinicalnews.org/on-location/ash-sickle-cell-disease-summit-a-call-to-action/
2. CISCRP and the ASH Research Collaborative to Engage Sickle Cell Disease Community CISCRP, March 25, 2019 https://www.ciscrp.org/collaboration-with-research-collaborative/
3. "NIH and National Foundation Expenditures For Sickle Cell Disease and Cystic Fibrosis Are Associated With Pubmed Publications and FDA Approvals" John J. Strouse, Katie Lobner, Sophie Lanzkron, MHS and Carlton Haywood Jr. Blood 2013 122:1739; http://www.bloodjournal.org/content/122/21/1739?sso-checked=true
4. CDC Clarifies Guideline on Opioid Prescribing for Chronic Pain Physician's Weekly, Apr 12, 2019 https://www.physiciansweekly.com/cdc-clarifies-guideline-on-opioid-prescribing-for-chronic-pain/
5. Hospitals See No Link Between US Opioid Crisis and Patients' Use of Treatment, Study Reports" Sickle Cell Anemia News, Jose Marques PHD, JANUARY 3, 2019 https://sicklecellanemianews.com/2019/01/03/opioid-abuse-not-seen-in-in-hospital-death-rates/
6. "Opioid crisis adds to pain of Sickle Cell patients." NIH, NHLBI September 15, 2017 https://www.nhlbi.nih.gov/news/2017/opioid-crisis-adds-pain-sickle-cell-patients
7. "Gene Therapy Advances Offer Hope for Sickle-Cell Disease Cure." WBUR, On Point, January 28, 2019 https://amp.wbur.org/onpoint/2019/01/28/sickle-cell-disease-gene-therapy

8. "Can Sickle Cell Disease Be Used as A Weapon Against Cancerous Tumors? New Study Says Yes" New York (CBS New York) April 29, 2019. https://newyork.cbslocal.com/2019/04/29/sickle-cell-disease-cancer-tumors/
9. "Can Sickle Cell Disease Be Used As A Weapon Against Cancerous Tumors? New Study Says Yes." New York(CBS New York) April 29, 2019 https://newyork.cbslocal.com/2019/04/29/sickle-cell-disease-cancer-tumors/
10. Project ECHO: A Revolution in Medical Education and Care Delivery https://echo.unm.edu/
11. Sickle Cell Disease and Project ECHO® "Connecting Providers and Experts to Improve Care, Outcomes and Costs." https://www.nichq.org/sites/default/files/inline-files/Project_ECHO_.pdf

CHAPTER 2

LET THE GOOD TIMES ROLL

HYDROXYUREA

We all know hydroxyurea. If you are in healthcare and dealing with Sickle Cell patients, you are taught about hydroxyurea as the knight in shining armor that supposedly came on the scene to whisk away all the Sickle Cell troubles of patients. For about two decades, it was the only treatment option for Sickle Cell disease. Cystic Fibrosis, another inherited disease that reduces life expectancy, and is only a third as common, got five drugs researched and created during this same period. But we had hydroxyurea, for *all* the Sickle Cell genotypes. [1,2]

Hydroxyurea is made by the pharmaceutical companies Bristol-Myers Squibb, Par Pharmaceutical, and Teva Pharmaceutical.[3] It was previously used as an oral cancer drug to treat certain leukemias and skin cancers. Accidentally, the chemotherapy agent was found to increase the levels of fetal hemoglobin[2] and was subsequently shared, to be also used in the treatment of Sickle Cell disease, which up until 1998 had no single treatment. NOT ONE!

Sickle Cell disease has been around since 1910 and was figured out to be a "molecular disease" by Linus Pauling in 1949.[4] Stop and think about that lapse between discovery and treatment for a minute...wow! Had it not been for this accidental finding, we would not even have Hydroxyurea. But I digress...

Hydroxyurea increases the levels of fetal hemoglobin, and this is good for one main reason. When we are born, we have fetal hemoglobin, also called hemoglobin F (Hg F), and it does not code for Sickle Cell. Because of this, the red blood cells carry oxygen beautifully! At some point during infancy, our blood transitions to "adult hemoglobin," and it is the adult hemoglobin that can cause sickling of the red blood cells. Hydroxyurea's exact mechanism of action for induction of fetal hemoglobin remains incompletely understood, but it seems to cause some sort of suppression of red blood cells causing stress in the bone marrow and resulting in elevated levels of HgF.[2]

Unfortunately, it is often only a small percentage of red blood cells that are switched off from making adult hemoglobin. For effective treatment, the goal is usually around 20 percent. In my case, the fetal hemoglobin raised to about 7 percent at best— a nice jump from the 0.6 percent of fetal hemoglobin that can be found in the general population.[5] However, for this modest rise, there were serious side effects on my health from the medication. After about two years, every person close to me was asking me to stop the medication, which I faithfully took.

I had several friends who were really helped by using Hydroxyurea, and I did not want to be the only one it didn't work for in my circle. Besides, I wanted a better quality of life for myself.

I was in medical school and desperately needed something to get me through those awful daily aches and excruciating pain flares. Nonetheless, my oncologist readily agreed that he was seeing more of the side effects than the benefits for me. He too decided it was time to stop the medication.

Alas, I could not sing the praises like everyone else around me. I subsequently learned that most of the studies conducted for the use of hydroxyurea were for the Sickle SS genotype. [6] The efficacy of the drug has not been well studied for us double heterozygotes like SC, S Beta-thalassemia zero, S Beta-thalassemia plus, all relatively common genotypes. Nor has it been done for the rarer genotypes of SD, SE and so on.

This is not to say that Hydroxyurea cannot work in these genotypes. In fact, I'm sure it has! It is simply to say that one medication often will not work for everyone. It sucks when you're compliant, but success was not meant to be.

In many cases, one size just cannot fit all. Take the case of leukemia for example. A variation in the type of leukemia can completely change the treatment needed, even though all leukemias affect the white blood cell line. I suspect there is much to be learned about how a variation in the genotype of our red blood cells can influence the type of treatment needed in Sickle Cell disease.

ENDARI

Endari is a new treatment specifically designed for Sickle Cell disease. Finally, over a century later, a treatment made just for us! Take a moment to digest that. It was released in 2017 and is created by Emmaus Pharmaceuticals.[7] This is not really a medication but a treatment, nonetheless. It is a known supplement prepared in a super-concentrated form. The only ingredient L-glutamine is a big-time antioxidant, a naturally occurring amino acid produced mainly by the lungs. Nice! Supplements! We like supplements, right?

In Sickle Cell disease, red blood cells become rigid due to oxidative stress. In this state, these cells become sticky and wreak havoc by attaching to each other, to the endothelial lining of blood vessels, to white blood cells and platelets. This often leads to blockage of blood circulation in that vein, otherwise known as a vaso-occlusive crisis, often with a sad outcome of tissue death and end-organ damage. L-glutamine being a potent antioxidant attempts to reverse this stress on these cells.

The body naturally makes this amino acid in smaller physiological quantities, but with sickling, we would need massive doses to overcome the overwhelming oxidation these sickled cells are experiencing.[7,8] The mega dose of antioxidant in the form of Endari is meant to slow down the process whereby the cells become oxidized and rigid.

But why L-glutamine as the antioxidant? This goes back to what's different about the DNA of the hemoglobin in Sickle Cell disease. At one point in the chain, there was supposed to be a coding for glutamic acid or glutamate. Instead, there was a substitution of valine and no glutamate.[7,8] See where this is going?

No glutamate? Okay, find some L-glutamate. Pour it on thick and step back. The body is one smart machine. Hopefully, things will sort themselves out. Turns out it is, and it does!

A lot of people I know have started on Endari with significant reductions in the frequency of their crisis pains and hospitalizations after some months of being on the treatment. Many have been helped. Many like me, are still waiting for the right match of treatment. My body never even gave the preparation a chance. I immediately experienced body aches as a side effect, which kept repeating itself with each try to my dismay. Nonetheless, I am genuinely happy for those receiving help.

I am an active member of several Sickle Cell support groups online, a few having upwards of 20,000 members. Even if it were only half this number of members with Sickle Cell disease, this sample size is still larger than any study I have seen for Sickle Cell disease. Thousands are invested to the point of sharing their experiences freely with respect to treatments and what is or isn't working for them. We all share. No one is above anyone. So, the truth comes out. Exciting times ahead!

CRIZANLIZUMAB

Crizanlizumab is made by Novartis. It is being made as a monthly infusion to be used for the treatment of Sickle Cell disease and will be given at a treatment center. Right now, Novartis is apparently working on the price point because currently, it is a rather expensive infusion.

The best way to explain the physiology of this drug is to have you picture a long hallway that represents the vascular system. Imagine students walking up and down that hallway and stopping to talk with each other as they walk past one another. Eventually, some students will congregate and block parts of the hallway because of clustering together.

That is the way that sickled cells normally work in our circulation, sticking together with each other and on the platelets, cells of the inflammation cascade, and even the walls of the endothelium. They can do this because on the surface of each cell, including the endothelial cells, red cells, white cells, and platelets is something called P-selectin, a molecule on the cell's surface that allows them to cling to each other in this way. [10] Think of them as having a strip of Velcro that snags on each other. The P-selectin on the cells makes the cells "select" each other, if that helps you remember. This sticking together blocks circulation and in turn, leads to tissue death.

Crizanlizumab is a protein that blocks this surface molecule on the cells, making the cells unable to stick to each other and cause vaso-occlusion.[9,10] It blocks the Velcro. Suddenly your sickled cells are not sticking to each other, they are not sticking to platelets or white blood cells and not sticking to the endothelial lining of your blood vessels. They are all smoothly passing by each other, and greatly reducing the possibility of vaso-occlusive crisis.

I have read that studies with the drug both at a low-dose and a high dose along a placebo group showed that the drug was dose-dependent in decreasing the number of episodes, with the high dose group decreasing the number of Sickle Cell crises a patient had and reducing the number of crises by 45% per year per patient. The study also noted that the interval between crises were greatly reduced as well.[9]

That's impressive data! I can't wait to see how we experience this drug as a community; I wish us well. From what I'm reading, it should be on the market by 2020.

VOXELOTOR

Voxelotor is an oral formulation made by a company called Global Blood Therapeutics.[11] The claim is that the drug can make oxygen bind preferentially to the hemoglobin in such a way that the hemoglobin molecule is always oxygenated. This is because it doesn't allow complete offloading of all the molecules of oxygen when releasing them to the tissues. [11,12] Let's just say it appears to save some oxygen bound to the hemoglobin for a rainy day.

Oxygen can bind to each of the four globin chains that make up hemoglobin as blood receives oxygen from the lungs. But apparently with Voxelotor, the hemoglobin is only releasing two or three of those molecules of oxygen to any given tissue or organ in the body upon the blood's arrival to the area. Because at least one molecule of oxygen seems to be always left bound to the hemoglobin, the hemoglobin is essentially always in an oxygenated state, and the cells are much less likely to sickle or become rigid and clog our vessels.[11,12]

Now, the thought here is that only in a completely deoxygenated state is the molecule of hemoglobin going to sickle.[11,12] So, as long as the chances for complete deoxygenation is reduced, there is less likelihood of irreversible sickling. Overall, there is an increased percentage of oxygenated red blood cells in the body's supply of blood.

This apparently also prevents the red blood cells from becoming damaged, since the hemoglobin does not sickle and become rigid often. Many more red blood cells are spared from their shortened lifespan of 10 to 30 days that is the usual fate of a sickled cell. And where there are more red blood cells, there is less anemia and all that comes with it. So, less fatigue, fewer episodes of overwhelming bone pain, and less incidence of organ damage. It is exciting to think that a drug can intercept the problem right where it starts, at the initial polymerization.[11,12]

Shut it down, and the body can stop screaming murder. And we warriors will happily leave those emergency rooms. Because we never wanted to be there in the first place! We have always wanted to be thrivers, not presumed drug-seekers. I suspect we don't always want to be "Sickle Cell warriors" either, because truthfully, we seek peace, not war.

For people like me who have had so much pulmonary compromise from the effects of sickling and scarring in my lungs, and walk around with supplemental oxygen always in tow, it would be nice to finally give the lung a chance to heal. With the normalization of my scarred, thickened alveoli, there would be an increase in the diffusion capacity of my oxygen again. I would no longer need portable oxygen wherever I go.

My Portable Oxygen Concentrator (POC) has become like another appendage. When I attended a symposium this summer (2019), I was blessed to be on a patient panel with a young preacher. Later, he approached me to share his good news of being an early recipient of the drug Voxelotor even before the clinical trials, on the grounds of compassionate care. He relayed to me that he was hardly able to walk previously, as he struggled with breathlessness from extensive sickling in his lungs. What stood out as a beacon of hope for me was the fact that his story was so much like mine!

He had no other lung pathology, no bronchial damage or other obstructive pulmonary disease to speak of, and no hypertension. He simply had extensive scarring in his lung parenchyma from years and years of attack by those sickled cells. There was no other source of restrictive lung disease. So essentially what I heard was "oxygenate my hemoglobin, save my lungs, save my body, save the world!"

Mr. Preacher was so excited for me! He took me by the hand and led me directly to the team of researchers and collaborators of Voxelotor from Global Blood Therapeutics. He made sure that we exchanged business cards and connected. I don't think he knew how much hope he left me with.

Voxelotor is being developed as a once in a day oral therapy. The FDA has allowed Voxelotor to be fast-tracked, with orphan drug and rare disease designation for the treatment of patients with Sickle Cell disease.[11]

Just for us. It's about time.

References

1. "NIH and National Foundation Expenditures for Sickle Cell Disease and Cystic Fibrosis Are Associated with Pubmed Publications and FDA Approvals." John J. Strouse, Katie Lobner, Sophie Lanzkron, MHS and Carlton Haywood Jr. Blood 2013 122:1739; http://www.bloodjournal.org/content/122/21/1739?sso-checked=true
2. Hydroxyurea in Sickle Cell Disease: Drug Review Rohit Kumar Agrawal, Rakesh Kantilal Patel, Varsha shah, Lalit Nainiwal, and Bhadra Trivedi Indian J Hematol Blood Transfus. 2014 Jun; 30(2): 91–96. https://www.ncbi.nlm.nih.gov/pmc/articles/PMC4022916/
3. Important Information Regarding Supply of Hydroxyurea American Society of Hematology November 09, 2011 https://www.hematology.org/Advocacy/Policy-News/2011/922.aspx
4. A Century of Progress: Milestones in Sickle Cell Disease Research and Care U.S Department of Health and Human Services, National Institutes of Health, September 2010 https://www.nhlbi.nih.gov/files/docs/public/blood/Tagged2NHLBISickleCellTimeline.pdf
5. Fetal hemoglobin levels in adults. Rochette J, et al. Blood Rev. 1994. https://www.ncbi.nlm.nih.gov/m/pubmed/7534152/
6. Effects of hydroxyurea treatment for patients with hemoglobin SC disease. Luchtman- Jones L, et al. Am J Hematol. 2016. https://www.ncbi.nlm.nih.gov/m/pubmed/26615793/
7. "FDA approves Emmaus' Endari to treat Sickle Cell disease" PHARMACEUTICAL TECHNOLOGY, 10 JULY 2017 https://www.pharmaceutical-technology.com/news/newsfda-approves-emmaus-endari-to-treat-sickle-cell-disease-5866958/

8. Endari (L-glutamine) for Sickle Cell Disease" SICKLE CELL ANEMIA NEWS, JULY 7, 2017 https://sicklecellanemianews. com/endari-l-glutamine/

9. "Effect of crizanlizumab on pain crises in subgroups of patients with Sickle Cell disease: A SUSTAIN study analysis." Kutlar A, et al. Am J Hematol. 2019 Jan; 94 (1):55-61.

10. FDA grants breakthrough therapy status to crizanlizumab PHARMACEUTICAL TECHNOLOGY 9 JANUARY 2019 https:// www.pharmaceutical-technology.com/news/fda-breakthrough-novartis-crizanlizumab/

11. "About Voxelotor in Sickle Cell Disease" Global Blood Therapeutics https://www.gbt.com/programs/scd/voxelotor/

12. "HOPE Trial Shows Voxelotor May Increase Hemoglobin, Reduce Anemia in Adults and Adolescents With SCD" Alice Melão, SICKLE CELL ANEMIA NEWS Jun 20, 2019 https:// sicklecellanemianews.com/2019/06/20/voxelotor

CHAPTER 3

BREAKTHROUGH

BONE MARROW TRANSPLANT:

A bone marrow transplant at one point was the only definitive cure for Sickle Cell Disease. It did come at the cost of needing a full sibling match (same mother and father) to reduce any chance of rejection of the donated bone marrow, or Graft Versus Host Disease (GVHD). HLA matching had to be very tight.[1,2]

HLA or Human Leukocyte Antigens are proteins located on the membranes of most of our cells that help our body determine what cells belong to the body and what cells are foreign and should be attacked if they tried to invade the body. In bone marrow or any other organ transplant, HLA proteins also determine whether certain cells or tissues are going to be compatible with each other, and which are not likely to be compatible. It's very difficult to find a perfect match because of this.[2]

However, bone marrow transplants have been successful in quite a few cases, and these recipients are often plastered on the television and in the newspapers and magazines to give us hope. Over the years with the perfection of the techniques people have been transplanted with only a partial sibling match![3] And last I checked at the University of Illinois, speaking directly with Dr. Damiano Rondelli, the upper limit for that transplant is age 60 years old, providing you can get your insurance to cover the procedure.

GENE THERAPY:

Gene therapy is the new dawn of Sickle Cell disease management and is the talk of the Sickle Cell community to be sure! It is hope on a silver platter to many of us, even while knowing that the technology is so very young with the kinks needing to be worked out.

With gene therapy, the wonderful thing is that we don't have to manipulate the patient's bone marrow to match anything, because we are using their bone marrow! What researchers and clinical scientists are now doing instead is looking at the mutation of DNA at the point on the beta hemoglobin and correcting the DNA right at that location. So, for Sickle Cell disease, it is position six on the beta hemoglobin. As you may recall, at this position there is an incorrect DNA coding where valine is placed instead of glutamic acid.[7]

Right now, there are three main ways in which scientists are addressing the gene-editing needed for Sickle Cell disease:

The first option is to leave in the wrong base pair(valine) and simply add the correct base pair (glutamic acid, or glutamate) in the hope that it would incorporate, encode and correct the error at position six of the beta hemoglobin on the DNA. Once this has occurred, they replicate this piece of DNA, insert it into a virus, and they allow the virus to enter the cells of the bone marrow.[4]

You are then given some chemotherapy to die off some of your native bone marrow so that it will not outgrow the corrected bone marrow, and then the corrected cells are transplanted giving it a chance to grow and populate the bone marrow space.

This new marrow now codes for the corrected beta hemoglobin, and the disease disappears!

The challenge with this type of gene therapy is that the coding is for a bigger stretch of DNA since they did not remove the valine but simply added glutamic acid next to it. Bigger is not always better.

The second type of gene therapy looks at hemoglobin F or fetal hemoglobin. Since it is not mutated, the function of the red blood cell is therefore normal. They "switch off" the production of Hemoglobin A, or adult hemoglobin, which has the mutation, and instead "switch on" the production of fetal hemoglobin.[5,6] This is done to a sample of the patient's bone marrow cells, and chemotherapy is given in the same way as the first option to prevent your native bone marrow from competing. Now, these corrected cells grow with the "switches" permanently reversed to make fetal hemoglobin always.

The third type is simply a variation of the first. Instead of just adding an extra glutamic acid while leaving the incorrectly substituted valine, they remove the valine by splicing it off and "pasting in" the glutamic acid.[4] The rest of the process is the same.

When I said we are enjoying a time of discovery and focus, I really meant it! I cannot think of any other time in the history of my disease that I have felt so optimistic. I recognize that, as is the nature of most drugs on the market, one size will not fit all. I am also keenly aware that much more testing tends to happen with genotype SS than my genotype SC. While it does make sense, it often makes my dream of treatment for my genotype seem deferred as I, along with all the other non-SS genotypes wait a few more years for our turn.

So far, I have shown you the very best side possible of Sickle Cell disease. Sincerely, it would be so nice to stop here and end the book. However, you could have easily fished out this information from the literature yourself. While it is nice to have the data at your fingertips with the exhaustive searches done for you, this is not my purpose for being here with you.

The unfortunate truth is that despite the picture of celebration I have just painted, this is where the excitement stops for the majority of patients with Sickle Cell disease-in a "picture" of hope. It is a beautiful picture, but not our past or current reality. Unfortunately, poor management of our Sickle Cell disease threatens to affect our future, possibly disqualifying us from being eligible for some of these treatments.

Permit me to explain how, because it involves you too.

References

1. American Cancer Society. Stem cell transplant (peripheral blood, bone marrow and cord blood transplants) Accessed 2/14/2014.
2. "HLA basics" BE THE MATCH. National Marrow Donor Program https://bethematch.org/transplant-basics/matching-patients-with-donors/
3. "Partial transplant reverses Sickle Cell" NIH trial success suggests a new treatment option for older, sicker patients OUR WEEKLY, July10, 2014 https://www.ourweekly.com/news/2014/jul/10/partial-transplant-reverses-sickle-cell/
4. "These Patients Had Sickle-Cell Disease. Experimental Therapies Might Have Cured Them." Gina Kolata, New York Times Jan. 27, 2019 https://www.nytimes.com/2019/01/27/health/sickle-cell-gene-therapy.html
5. "New gene therapy strategy for Sickle Cell disease shows early promise in humans" Dana-Farber Cancer Institute DECEMBER 01, 2018.
6. In A 1st, Doctors In U.S. Use CRISPR Tool To Treat Patient With Sickle Cell Disease, National Public Radio July 29, 2019 https://www.npr.org/sections/health-shots/2019/07/29/744826505/sickle-cell-patient-reveals-why-she-is-volunteering-for-landmark-gene-editing-st 19)
7. "How Does Sickle Cell Cause Disease? The Mutation in Hemoglobin" April 11,2002 Sickle.bwh.harvard.edu/scd_background.html

ALL RISE!

Part 2

CHAPTER 4

WOUNDS MUST HEAL

It hurts on some level to believe that a book like this needs to exist. My Sickle Cell disease journey has been one of heartache that ended in triumph and has had me dancing giddily because I finally realized that what I, along with the rest of the world, had seen as an obstacle was turning out to be my journey to self-acceptance and embracing my divine purpose. So, I wanted my story of overcoming and "beauty for ashes" to have a lovely bow tied neatly around it.

The dilemma I have is that framing it this way would necessitate ignoring wounds that could never fully heal until they were aired, washed, and properly dressed with the right salve. To ignore these parts would not only minimize my pain, but it would silence a community of Sickle Cell sufferers who are begging to be heard, aching to be reassured that someone is listening and will eventually do something. They are waiting to have their pain validated by the medical community, and more importantly, to be treated adequately in their times of anguish and vulnerability.

So, it is with great reluctance that I must expose the ugly side of an otherwise well-respected establishment, so that perhaps, just perhaps, we might begin to properly treat it, and heal.

I have matured greatly in handling my own regrets when it comes to life with Sickle Cell. My days of bitterness and utter frustration are now seldom and flanked by a little more understanding as I have had to navigate this medical profession, where people put doctors on a pedestal and then enjoy watching them fall from it. I have had time to reflect on my medical disappointments and grieve about the way my health was sometimes poorly managed over the years. Today I can frame those hurts with the grander picture of spiritual wholeness and the blessing of a new purpose.

But I did not arrive there with velocity. So, when I listen to the masses of Sickle Cell sufferers all wailing the same words of despair about their poor treatment, amazed and disgusted by the ignorance of professionals towards their pain and plight, I understand. I know that it is not an imagined story when I hear my account of an experience from the mouth of a patient from Texas, who shares a similar narrative as someone from Chicago, or any other place. It is for this reason that I cannot tell a decidedly happy story. It would not only be inconsiderate; it would be extremely wrong.

I have chosen to speak on those things I can verify, namely, my own health history. I have chosen those experiences of mine that seem to be echoed from the mouths of other Sickle Cell patients in every support group or chat that I am part of. Let me reassure you, there is no paucity of content. Indeed, I wish there was because that would mean that most of my hospitalizations were smooth and without regret. Unfortunately, this was not my portion.

The goal, however, is not to bash nurses or doctors, as I would hope that my patients would never do that to me. Neither is it to exonerate every Sickle Cell patient. We must admit that as patients, we have sometimes made assumptions against even the most well-meaning providers, and hurt them in a way that may have permanently affected their perspective and our care. My goal instead is to present various cases that may highlight some degree of ineptitude or lack of knowledge, and either explain why this might indeed be the case, *or* show that things are not as they appear.

I hope that by the time we are through, not only will the travails of Sickle Cell be familiar to you, but also the changes needed to create a more welcoming healthcare experience. It is also my greatest wish that you will allow me to propose some solutions from my journey with Sickle Cell disease. I am hoping that my vulnerability can provide insight that can help us as a community of healthcare providers to approach a better standard of care for this disenfranchised patient population.

CHAPTER 5

PREVENTION VS. "CURE"

I had been watching my health fall apart in slow motion for quite a while, and the other shoe had just dropped. Oh, how I wish we had followed the protocol we talked about with my orthopedic doctor back then! It took me a long time emotionally to stop hurting over how that one decision affected my life.

Nice doctors don't automatically make good doctors. You know enough to know this by now. Things can happen, and people can get hurt. It was "nice doctors" who had overlooked other problems in my health history, with every symptom attributed only to Sickle Cell. This time, it was all because we missed that ounce of prevention after my first hip surgery in the form of post-operative antibiotics.

I remember the first time we met with Dr. S in his office. He was tall, like most orthopedic surgeons, and looked quite distinguished. His deep voice made me believe everything he said to us. I remember that we were crammed into his exam room - the orthopedic surgeon, me and my husband Aniekan, along with my "San Francisco adopted parents," as I seemed to have had one in every city I lived. They were worried about what was about to happen next, as they should have been. Jan had stood many times beside me in the emergency room. She had also accompanied me for many other medical visits to my other doctors, and despite her gentle disposition, her Caucasian status spoke loudly to my doctors that I mattered, and somebody loved me enough to be watching over me. To me, she was "mom Jan," friend and sister in Christ. To them, she represented caution.

"I don't have a lot of Sickle Cell cases, so you're going to be treated right. We're going to make sure everybody's on board. And we're going to start you on post-surgical prophylactic IV antibiotics. Since your immune system is suppressed with your steroids, we'll to have to help you fight. I suspect your recuperation might not be the same length of time as everyone else; probably going to be longer since you all (referring to Sickle Cell patients) tend to have delayed healing it seems. So, we will have to watch for that." I remember feeling very taken care of.

I look back now and wished things had not gone so downhill. To begin with, the whole surgery became more complicated because, between the hematologists and the orthopedic team, neither one would take responsibility for when they should stop my blood thinners before the surgery and when they should restart it. Sadly, it caused extensive post-surgical bleeding. To add insult to injury, someone in the chain of command forgot about starting the post-operative prophylactic IV antibiotics. So, for the entire nine days that I was hospitalized post-surgically as they dealt with the bleeding complications and impact on wound healing, I received no IV antibiotics, and was not discharged with any either!

And that one thing cost me not just my quality of life, but ultimately my medical practice!

I remember that soon after the surgery, my biological mom appeared and wanted to be very hands-on. What she did not realize was that her voice would be less heard. Furthermore, despite her best efforts, she was not as updated on the situation as my "adopted mother" and did not always know the questions to ask or situations to address. Because she lived in another state, she was also not present during the preop visits, so she was not aware of the promises made to me in that exam room with my husband and "adopted parents."

My husband was unfortunately a shell of himself during this time, mourning the loss of his aunt, a woman who had been like a second mother to him during pivotal moments of his life, including the years after the untimely passing of his beautiful soul of a mother. He had reached his emotional limit. He came back to San Francisco, from Maryland, convinced that there were too many cooks involved in my care, and with my fragile health, something terrible could happen. His sorrow made him present in body but absent in mind for my first hip surgery.

To further complicate matters, as brilliant as he is, because he is dark in complexion, and has a mild Nigerian accent, it often resulted in misjudgment from my doctors. Because my husband is so well-mannered, he did not react to many of these things. Furthermore, he was too emotionally invested to think straight. So, the only ones monitoring or holding the doctors accountable were the doctors themselves. Not the best set up of checks and balances, it was frustrating. But Dr. S. was such a nice man!

It was a long and complicated surgery that resulted in me bleeding into the spaces between my skin and muscle. At one point, my leg appeared as though I had elephantiasis. It almost seemed like a separate entity from my body; it was enormously huge. The skin was shiny and glistening from being so stretched to accommodate the massive volume of blood trapped in the tissues of my leg. A wave of pain arose from my hip soon after surgery followed by the onset of a Sickle Cell crisis, likely triggered by the stress of dropping blood counts as I bled into my leg.

So, with as much as I had vying for my attention, I did not notice that very important thing called antibiotics missing from the protocol. In fact, it was only after that lengthy post-surgical stay and getting home that I realized the home health nurse showing up had no IV antibiotics! In my pain delirium, I did not think to message the doctor, so our clinic follow-up would be the next time we could address this, and it was now approaching two weeks!

My doctor finally started oral cephalexin after being reminded by me at my first post-op visit. "Oh, that's right!" he dryly admitted. "Well, no problem, we can still start it now. Oral cephalexin is just as "bioavailable" as IV cephalexin, so let's go with that." And that was that! As harrowing an experience as I had endured since the surgery, it was the first time I recalled being disappointed.

The wound, which had been stapled shut instead of sutured, kept bleeding out from every staple into the surgical dressing, just like it had been doing since the surgery. I don't mean oozing either; it simply gushed blood. And it never stopped. Because it hurt my buttocks to sit upright, someone had bought a doughnut-shaped cushion that appeared to be filled with cotton. I could position my buttock into the middle of the cushion and be somewhat lifted from the surface of the chair.

One of the most embarrassing things I will ever remember was with that cushion. I was sitting up to receive my visitors, friends who were there for us through the crazy days. Toward the end of what was likely an hour-long visit, my friend Valerie came to hug me goodbye. Suddenly, there was a loud cry from her as she very frantically pointed down to my cushion. In the time we had been talking, my wound had briskly bled out and into the cotton-filled cushion. It was such a bright red, and it looked as though I had a monster of a menstrual accident! But it was all coming from the eighteen-inch wound in my left lateral thigh.

It was not rocket science when I started having fevers of 103 degrees Fahrenheit soon after and woke up one morning with excruciating pain in the hip. It had become infected barely over three weeks after surgery, and oozing pus when they aspirated the joint.

I ended up with a second hip surgery just barely over a month later. It would have been sooner, but my orthopedic surgeon was out of the country, and there was great disagreement amongst the covering team about what should be done. So, we waited for his return. After the second surgery, I was prescribed IV antibiotics like it was water.

Six months later, after trying to control whatever residual infection was present, they stopped the IV antibiotics. And within weeks, the bugs were back. Truth was, they had never left from the very first time when they seeded into my joint. So yes, you guessed it! My third hip surgery was only ten months from my first. An ounce of prevention with immediate IV antibiotics really would have been better than the pound of cure of THREE HIP SURGERIES IN TEN MONTHS! They had learned their lesson. But ultimately, I was paying the price.

After my third surgery, everyone was on high alert and had gotten the memo loud and clear about the need for isolating the bug and creating an IV antibiotic treatment therapy. They were very remorseful about the fact that these multiple surgeries had caused the surrounding hip capsule to become weak, with the hip becoming loose and dislocating on multiple occasions, causing chaotic runs to the emergency room and several admissions.

They also realized that because I relapsed so quickly after six months of IV antibiotics therapy, I must have some deep-seated bugs in my hip. And they wanted no chances of it coming back. Their solution? Lifetime oral antibiotic therapy! Yes, you heard me right - a lifetime of being on antibiotics that could create many strains of resistant bacteria in my body.

And that was my only choice, take it or leave it.

I relocated to Orlando, Florida the following year. My health, having been adequately traumatized with three surgeries in less than a year, rigorous antibiotic therapies, and several hip dislocations resulting in hip bleeds and hospitalizations, was officially wrecked. And after all those dislocations, they finally recommended something called a "hip brace."

My body was not bouncing back like it used to, and I was unable to walk properly, much less practice medicine. I was now also boasting a leg length discrepancy after the surgeries. I was on disability, collecting a fraction of my salary. I felt like my only hope of returning to my medical practice was to salvage whatever I had left of my health by taking a year off and moving to a warmer climate that would be helpful to my now fragile health. That warmer place turned out to be Orlando.

I remember before leaving asking Dr. S if he knew of any good orthopedic surgeons in Orlando.

His reply was, "don't let anyone else touch that hip!" If anything happens, fly back to me and let me do the surgery.

I would not understand the ridiculousness of that advice until three years later, when the need arose as I walked into the emergency room of a major trauma center. I knew full well upon waking up that day that my hip had become septic, AGAIN! And on a double antibiotic regimen! Who was going to get on a plane and fly across the country like that?

Another doctor later explained to me that maybe they were not proud of the work that they had done on my hip or the mistakes that had been made. Maybe they just did not want another surgeon to see what had actually happened. I honestly don't know what the reason was for that advice.

The surgeon in Orlando was also a tall, handsome man with a reassuring voice. But this time, I was not swayed by that in the least. I remember the Orthopedic resident speaking to me in the ER and asking, almost shouting, "who the ****! puts a patient on lifetime antibiotics and leaves the infection in the hip? Why didn't they just take out all the ****! hardware from the hip, clean out the space, and start over with a new hip?" He was hot! And his anger at my travesty was being directed to...me?

He continued, "Obviously just washing out the joint space and the hardware did not work the first time (referring to my second surgery) so why the ****! do it again (referring to my third surgery)! It takes about four to six months to bounce back, but ****, at least it would be over with! And you wouldn't be tearing up your gut and immune system with these ****! Antibiotics. Truth is at some point these bugs were going to become resistant to the antibiotics anyway. It was just a matter of time!"

I just sat there feeling rather silly for someone else's mistake in treatment, like somehow, I was supposed to stand up to my previous orthopedic team of surgeons and give them pointers on how best to treat a septic hip! I was not a surgeon or on the infectious disease team!

Truth is, the resident standing there, venting his frustration on my behalf had lost me at the utterance of "six months." Because when I heard that it would take six months to finally fix the mess in my hip, knowing my history of Sickle Cell disease and how it responds under these circumstances, something in my spirit broke. All I could think of was "I know it won't be six months! It's always double or more of whatever they say. Dear God! My medical career is over!"

Indeed, it was the straw that broke this camel's back. I was never able to practice medicine again.

46

What do I want you to take away from my painful experience? What can I teach you? My hope is that I can etch into your mind the absolute necessity for "prevention versus cure" in treating Sickle Cell disease. Don't wait to treat a crisis; look to prevent one! If treatment is needed, treat sooner not later! Honestly, our bodies usually do not tolerate casual, reactionary medicine. It responds badly to that kind of stress. Also, any invasive treatment should have antibiotic prophylaxis offered, if not before, then immediately after.

Some things will have poor outcomes, I get it. But let it be after you have done everything you knew to do beforehand. And whatever you do, always assume somebody is watching, or will eventually judge your handiwork. Because in the end, somebody *is* watching.

CHAPTER 6

MY THREE TYPES OF PAIN

I notice there is a pain component that the narcotic analgesic will barely touch. It can be compared to a lock and key situation, and using morphine is like using the wrong key for that pain lock. Very early on I noticed that addressing such things sometimes made a difference in the number of narcotic analgesics I needed, and my length of hospital stay.

Ischemic pain comprises most of my Sickle Cell pain. This is the same type of pain a person having a heart attack feels because essentially the same thing is going on, except with Sickle Cell disease, your entire body is having that "heart attack." As the tissues die, these areas will hurt or express that trauma in some way. It can happen wherever blood flows; the heart (myocardial ischemia, which I have felt) the lungs (caused me pulmonary infarcts), the hips or other bones(caused me bilateral avascular necrosis of hips and five surgeries), the kidneys(can lead to medullary infarcts), or the brain(caused me to have a mini-stroke or TIA).

When someone with a heart attack is taken to the emergency room, sometimes *even before* they arrive, they are given

49

morphine and oxygen for severe ischemic pain.[1] So too should Sickle Cell be treated for ischemic pain with morphine or other appropriate narcotics and oxygen since unlike the heart attack (of course serious in its own right), Sickle Cell pain is often multi-systemic and much harder to break.

My inflammatory pain is like the joint pain most people feel with arthritis or musculoskeletal pain. For the most part it feels like a reactionary pain to me, possibly in response to surrounding ischemic trauma I have had. An anti-inflammatory would be best suited, whether it is a steroid or an NSAID like Toradol. It's tricky since, because of the potential of serious renal compromise, Sickle Cell patients like me are not supposed to use over the counter NSAIDS.[2] For me, this is where my integrative medicine ideas work well. I assume I'm always experiencing some amount of inflammatory pain as a part of the sickling process.

I remember the days when I would say to my hematologists and pain specialists, "There has to be some micro angiopathic component of inflammation. I feel like I'm inflamed right after a crisis". I would beg to try COX2 inhibitors like Celebrex and anything else to decrease the need for narcotic analgesics because while they did not affect my memory, they caused such sedation. And who had time to sleep in medical school?! Meanwhile, my doctors would look at me like I had a third eye and say, "Simone, it's not an inflammatory disease. But...I guess it won't hurt to try some Celebrex." Those were the days. Like I say, "I live in this house, so I can feel what's going on much more than they."

The third type of pain I experience is neuropathic pain. It is not often a pain that people will associate with Sickle Cell disease, but if you think about it, it's most obviously has to be there.

Sickling and clogging of the blood vessels can happen in any part of the body. If those blood vessels were giving oxygen and nutrients to nerve tissue, and that circulation is cut off, the result can be damage to those nerves, which then leads to nerve pain or neuropathy.

This quite resembles the neuropathic pain that diabetics experience, with damage to the nerves in their hands and feet due to poor circulation. This is called peripheral nerve pain.[3]

However, once again, since our vaso-occlusion is multi-systemic, I have had nerve damage in quite some unusual places. Through my research on this and advocating for myself, I was finally given medications sometime in 2005 to help with neuropathic pain. This has greatly eased the burning pains I felt in my stomach and spine and elsewhere. And as a result, my breakthrough pains were less, and so was my use of short-acting narcotic analgesics.

Over the years as I experienced more wear and tear, the locations of my neuropathic pain increased. For example, my hip surgeries for avascular necrosis resulted in poor replacement of some of the surrounding muscles and tissues of the hip, exposing my sciatic nerve so much that I can no longer sleep on my left side, which is how I had always slept. Trying to sleep this way caused me to wake up screaming in pain because at some point, I angled in a way that aggravated the nerve and I felt like a blaze of fire had started on my thigh. The first time this happened, I sprang out of bed middle of the night looking for ice to douse my leg. Even after it was obvious the nerve had stopped firing, I still applied the ice because the overlying tissue felt burnt and sore. Of course, it was just my luck that the sudden exposure of all that cold started a pain crisis.

Obviously, in the case of my sciatica, it did not originate directly from the AVN but was a result of the surgery. I highlight this to explain that when you have surgeries and tissue planes are interrupted, this itself can cause neuropathy. Any trauma to the nerve for ANY reason can produce neuropathy. The difference is that because I have Sickle Cell disease, which is already painful, this pain can be overlooked, dwarfed by the Sickle Cell pain. Unfortunately, I realized that when these other components of my pain were not diagnosed and treated, the stress created by them often triggered my "sleeping giant" — Sickle Cell. I would end up with Sickle Cell pain triggered by a stress response, generated by continuous, unresolved nerve pain.

I was once readmitted after discharge for a Sickle Cell crisis because no one did a physical examination of my back on the first admission. It turns out I was having terrible nerve pain and inflammatory pain in my spine, likely caused by chronic intermittent sickling in my spine. In the past, I have had sickling in my spine cause necrosis and decompression that ultimately resulted in fractures and back surgery. So, it would have been a good move to examine my spine. If they had pressed on the spinal column, my reaction would have clued them (and me) in.

As it happened, the nerve/inflammatory pain triggered an acute Sickle Cell crisis. This was eventually controlled by IV medication during my first admission, and I was sent home. However, since the nerve pain and inflammatory pain were not treated, they re-triggered *another* Sickle Cell crisis, causing me to crawl back to the ER, as much as I hate that place. The second admission was even worse, and me being in pain just about everywhere, I did not clue in. I was again discharged, but not with my pain controlled at all. I knew the medications were not working, and with a shortage of Dilaudid, I thought to myself, "I will make it or I won't. I'm at peace."

My husband just happened to start massaging my back as I was sitting on the side of the bed after returning home, and a pain seared through my body. Only then did I realize what had likely happened. I reached for my EMLA cream-a lidocaine cream I'm prescribed for numbing the skin-and my husband gently smeared it in a thick strip up and down my back.

Thirty minutes later...sweet relief! I refilled my EMLA cream that day, called my oncologist and explained what I thought had happened. She called in prescription strength Lidocaine patches. By late evening the oral pain meds had controlled the crisis, and the lidocaine on my back had dulled the nerve pain to a pause. I slept like a baby that night.

References

1. "Infarction Treatment & Management" A Maziar Zafari, MD, PhD, FACC, FAHA et al. Medscape, The Heart.org May 07, 2019 https://emedicine.medscape.com/article/155919-treatment
2. "Use of Anti-inflammatory Analgesics in Sickle Cell Disease." Jin Han,[1,2,3,*] Santosh L. Saraf,[2] James P. Lash,[4] and Victor R. Gordeuk[2] J Clin Pharm Ther. 2017 Oct; 42(5): 656–660. https://www.ncbi.nlm.nih.gov/pmc/articles/PMC5774978/
3. "Guide to Diabetic Peripheral Neuropathy" WebMD 4-17-2018. https://www.webmd.com/diabetes/ss/slideshow-diabetic-peripheral-neuropathy#

CHAPTER 7

INTEGRATIVE MEDICINE

I'm a Family Practice Doctor by training. I have treated all ages, from the "womb to the tomb." My greatest joys were delivering babies into this world and turning some of the most tragic situations into happy endings.

But I'm an "Integrative Medicine mindset" doctor. I hate the way conventional medicine has gone with all the pill-popping! I was SO sure when I went to medical school that I would learn preventive strategies and holistic treatments, like some of our other first world countries. I went to some of the best schools in the country too!

I learned some natural strategies from international doctors that came during my preclinical years of medicine at Stanford and taught us what they were doing around the world. They showed us how to diagnose problems without access to fancy machine, but using our five senses, and maybe a stethoscope. This was right up my alley, as I grew up picking the plants that healed my body from my back yard in Guyana, South America.

But alas "Big Pharma" has funded many medical schools and seem to be suggesting to them what to include in the syllabus. It is why we never got along smoothly. I was not about to hide the truth from my patients when I knew something better that could help them. I am grateful for all the education that taught me the structure and function of every aspect of the human body and disease presentations. But how to heal the patient is where we diverged. I often took the path less traveled, at least for western medicine.

Now to be sure, Big Pharma is not the enemy. Many of us know that in some instances, medication is all we have. Many medicines have been made that treat and significantly change the lives of the people who needed them. When people end up with rare diseases that nothing can treat, and they hear of a clinical trial testing some experimental drug, they clamor to be enrolled in those studies for a chance to prolong their days on earth. So, we cannot speak about this industry out of both sides of our mouths.

However, I have never believed that one type of treatment would be the answer to everything. Yet, we frequently rely heavily on just pills. I had hoped we would have a symbiotic relationship with other disciplines of medicine, doing whatever worked for the patient. And I am grateful that at Stanford University School of Medicine, they at least gave me the choice of knowing these other fields of health care exist! In my time I have seen benefits with energy medicine, acupuncture, chiropractic care, naturopathic medicine and biofeedback, all with good nutrition on board.

But unfortunately, there is little partnership with these other options of health care. So, I was left disappointed, walking away, and hoping one day these entities would stop the fruitless and baseless fighting, and just "kiss and make up" for the benefit of the rest of us whose lives are at stake.

I wrote a piece about how I felt-regarding these health care providers working so separately-from a patient's perspective. It was called "The Forgotten Child."

"I feel terribly disappointed, betrayed and neglected that conventional medicine and holistic medicine could not find a way to work hand in hand peacefully so that I could grow and thrive in my beautifully blended integrative medicine family."

As someone with Sickle Cell disease, I found out the hard way that it is dangerous to only consider one discipline of medicine when you are desperate and looking for help. I did this for many years and suffered, treated with harsh narcotic medications which provided more sedation than analgesia, which had to be raised to the level of causing respiratory depression all in the name of trying to get my pain under control.

These whopping doses of IV Dilaudid, Fentanyl or Demerol (no longer used) made me hallucinate often, seeing my doctors and nurses as though they were walking around the hospital naked, as if I had some sort of x-ray vision. I had troubled dreams, feeling like I had traveled to a parallel universe where it seemed like children never grew old, and there was always a parade or celebration of some sort. Yet, I felt far from home and cried with relief when I woke up and realized that I had made it back. All because of these potent narcotic medications!

Meanwhile, they did little to stop the advancement of my disease, and so for all the times that I was admitted for the much-needed pain management, nothing got better. I watched in silent panic as my body's organs and tissues declined to the point of needing one surgery after another, and I was helpless in stemming the deterioration.

Or so I thought. I had been adequately brainwashed that conventional (western) medical practice options were all I had until I became desperate enough to start listening to the people around me who were enjoying relatively good health with other disciplines of medicine, like acupuncture, chiropractic care, energy medicine, functional medicine, and nutrition. These people were employing a holistic approach. And they were preventing disease progression instead of treating symptoms. It was quite a promising prospect for me. It reminded me of growing up in Guyana, where food was medicine. I wanted in!

First, someone taught me how to drink water.

I drink warm water when I first get out of bed and on cold days to keep my veins dilated, which keeps my red blood cells from sticking and clogging. I was told that different sizes of laundry need different amounts of water to wash it, and different sizes of people need different amounts of water to wash them. Using this analogy, I was encouraged to take the number of my body weight in pounds, divide it in two, and the number I got was the amount of water in ounces I needed to drink per day.

The next helpful thing I was told was that I needed to supplement with large doses vitamins and minerals-not your average store bought products- because of our foods and the nutrient-depleted soils they grow in.[1] The supply of nutrients that we need each day could never be met by our foods, at least not here in the USA. They are mass-produced and grown on overused farmlands. Because the lands get no chance to rest as farmers try to keep up with supply and demand, the grounds become depleted of vital nutrients. I was also made to understand from a well-known naturopathic doctor that, as someone with Sickle Cell disease, I am severely deficient in selenium, vitamin B6, and copper and should take extra doses of these daily. This is in addition to the daily repletion of the vital nutrients our body needs as raw materials to work[3].

Although I have more energy and feel better, I get no applause from my doctors even when they see me improving right before their eyes. There were no randomized case-controlled studies that I could cite, just positive feedback from the many people with Sickle Cell disease who changed their diet and improved their health. So, my doctors could not embrace this option, harmless as it was.

But I love being proactive about my health, especially when there are currently no effective treatments for me. Unfortunately though, I am not always able to use the things that really help me because nothing is covered by my insurance unless I am using conventional medicine. But conventional medicine is usually reactive medicine or emergency care, after the fact. It does not work with chronic care. I don't want to put out fires. I want to keep them from ever starting.

The third thing I was told was to watch my environment and what was getting into my body because of that environment. It could be the perfumes and lotions on my skin that have toxic substances but smell wonderful, or it could be the exposure to gasoline fumes at the gas station when I was already at risk with my limited lung capacity. It could be the water that I bathed with, and the high levels of chlorine the water has if there is no water softener system attached to the home.

Whatever it was, my goal was to make step by step changes that would decrease the introduction of threatening chemicals into my world, things that could suppress my immune system or cause oxidative stress in my body while battling a life-threatening illness. These were all things I could change naturally that would improve the quality of my life exponentially and without the addition of any pharmaceutical drug, along with potentially numerous side effects.

However, when I am acutely ill, conventional medicine comes to the rescue with its many benefits. If I am invaded by some bacteria with a rapidly worsening infection, please take me to the emergency room at once and start me on those pharmaceutical antibiotics, if necessary. I can rebalance my gut flora once I'm stabilized. If my blood pressure skyrockets and puts me at risk for a stroke, please use whatever pharmacologic concoction is available - clonidine, Lasix, whatever is needed, to stabilize and normalize me. I can possibly transition off these medicines or to lower dosages at a later time, as I balance my nutrition and pursue natural alternatives to address blood pressure.

If I am in a whopper of a sickle crisis, please give me the pain medications to minimize the stress response and, subsequently, the oxygen deprivation to my tissues. Afterward, I can return to preventive medicine and adjust things to reduce my chances of another pain crisis.

Every discipline of medicine has its place. But when I tried to marry the two disciplines of medicine - holistic and conventional - by encouraging my health care providers on each side to speak with each other, I got a level of pushback I had not expected. I felt like a child whose parents were divorced, with one parent dropping off the child (me) to another parent on the days that they had custody. Or worse, in their pride and intolerance of each other, they have left the child to navigate back-and-forth between them. I was in the middle, trying desperately to make them talk to each other, love each other, and work together.

At times I saw glimmers of hope when I heard of an M.D. using alternative methods, or a naturopathic doctor admitting that there is a place for a medical doctor in the areas of infectious disease treatment, emergency room care, or even for disease diagnoses. I was so excited when I heard that the NIH tried Reiki therapy (energy medicine).[2]

But most of the times, these providers in both the conventional and holistic disciplines act like grownup children, one not wanting the other to exist, and forgetting the child (patient) in the middle. Truthfully, the only mature person in the situation is the child, who can always see the beauty in both of them and is forever optimistic about a possible union.

References

1. Dirt Poor: Have Fruits and Vegetables Become Less Nutritious? Scientific American April 27, 2011 https://www.scientificamerican.com/article/soil-depletion-and-nutrition-loss/
2. "Reiki Is Better Than Placebo and Has Broad Potential as a Complementary Health Therapy." David E. McManus, PhD, Journal of Evidence-Based Complementary and Alternative Medicine
3. https://www.ncbi.nlm.nih.gov/pmc/articles/PMC5871310/
4. Epigenetics: The Death of the Genetic Theory of Disease Transmission by Wallach D.V.M, Joel D., Lan M.D., Ma, et al. p197-200 | May 10, 2014

CHAPTER 8

REGRETTABLE THINGS FOR HEALTH

The things I have done to survive have left me frightened, exhausted, and embarrassed. I should not have had to choose. I should not have been forced to choose. I didn't have time to go to the doctor because I am one!

Our lives are crazy, even for healthy people. So how does someone get hospitalized six to eight times a year, live in ache all year round, keep in step with a residency program, (and later a busy clinical practice) and keep all required doctors' appointments of all countless specialists? They don't. They have to cut corners somewhere.

I had a primary doctor, a hematologist for my Sickle Cell disease, and a cardiologist after having some cardiac events related to massive pulmonary emboli (blood clots in the lungs). These clots had caused the heart to strain as it pumped against the clogged arteries leading to my lungs. I had a pulmonologist for the multiple lung clots and scarring from sickling in the lung tissue. Then there was an endocrinologist because I had sickled in my adrenal glands and partially destroyed them. I now had to be on lifetime steroids to make up for the poor functioning of these glands.

I had an orthopedic hip surgeon for Avascular Necrosis of my hips that would eventually lead to multiple surgeries and an infectious disease specialist for the unfortunate post-surgical hip infection that occurred soon after. I needed an orthopedic spine surgeon because of fractures in my thoracolumbar spine that required back surgery. Then, there was a shoulder orthopedist because of tendon ruptures in my shoulder which they determined required surgery. These surgeons, just to keep my life exciting, had clinics in different locations!

As if I didn't have enough, there was a neurologist to keep track of lacunar infarcts, death of tiny areas of brain cells from lack of oxygen, in this case from sickling in the brain. Oh, and there was a sleep specialist for what turned out to be Central Sleep Apnea, poor signals from the brain causing me to stop breathing without any snoring and significantly decrease the oxygen saturation in my blood. Of course, that was triggering my Sickle Cell disease even further, because low oxygen tension causes these red blood cells to stress and sickle.

Now, of course, I was not spared from everyday health problems because I had a genetic disorder! However, even these health issues seemed more complicated than usual because of my primary diagnosis. So, the gynecologist tried to control the menstrual cycles that were wreaking havoc on my system. These monthly episodes were causing even further anemia from blood loss, and constantly triggering a Sickle Cell crisis, landing me in the hospital almost every month for a day or so.

The ophthalmologist monitored my eye vessels so she could spot any early signs of sickling there. Then, because I received my family's DNA with all the associated maladies as well, I saw an ENT specialist for an inherited chronic sinusitis. Did I mention the dentist? Yes, for whatever reason I had left to smile, I saw a dentist.

Yes, I think that might be everything! If you were exhausted reading this list, I was infinitely more exhausted living it! And that is exactly my point. Finding time to see every provider I needed to see to manage all these different issues was a nightmare. I also needed time off for MRIs and X-rays, or sometimes just for getting prescriptions refilled, since controlled substances had no refills and therefore needed monthly appointments. Likewise, other medications needed monitoring with blood work before another prescription could be written. Managing my health was turning out to be a whole other side job! Honestly, it was sheer madness!

As if I had any energy left, I was always "fighting" with someone. It started with my insurance, for coverage of everything from procedures to medications or any other treatment. I was negotiating (more like begging) with the scheduling person of every doctor's office to help me get in and out of an appointment, in a way that would be least intrusive to my residency schedule, and later the schedules of whichever practice I was working for. The only problem was that since I was often afraid to tell the schedulers that I was a practicing doctor with ALL that drama, I would not disclose why I needed to be given consideration during appointments.

Honestly, I was living a double life, and it was quickly becoming too much. Sickle cell disease and chronic pain management felt like two special needs children that I had wrongly tucked away from the public because I was somehow made to feel like it would be a liability. Based on my unfortunate experiences and learning the hard way, I knew that people would immediately question my loyalty to their team and my ability to show up wherever and whenever they needed me. I was scared that they would use my need for pain medications against me. It did not help that I continually was told to keep "that information" a secret lest we got sued by patients for frivolous things because they knew I was "vulnerable." So, I took care of these "liabilities" silently. And on the side, I practiced medicine.

I started my practice knowing that I could never work full time because someone would "smell a rat" too quickly. I needed too much time off to get too many things done each month. I usually zoomed right through my sick days and vacation days as it were. Just to put anyone who worked with me at ease at any time, I coined my little response to everyone that was cautious about me working - "Yes, I do have Sickle Cell disease, but I have SC."

Now, as you already know, my SC often behaved more like SS and at some points had me even sicker than some of the SS patients I knew, but why sink my own ship! And a girl can hope for the best, right?

I always informed employers about my Sickle Cell disorder. But my conversations went something like this:

"Because I'd like to be able to deliver to you on what I promise in terms of my availability, I would prefer to work three days a week. This leaves me with the time I need to optimize my health so that my problem never becomes yours. And when I'm here, I will be present to my patients and my work".

It usually was enough to pacify most people, and I did my darned best to make sure my two worlds did not collide. But inevitably the relationship soured, because someone who did not know my private dance between these two worlds would assume I had "extra time off" that was a disadvantage to the other colleagues, and would attempt to level the playing field by cherry-picking which patients they would have, leaving the hardest cases for me because, well, "I had time". And I always seemed to be the one asked to pick up the slack wherever that was because the others were "so busy already." And if someone could not make it in, it became, "Dr. Uwan would you mind covering for Dr. X? Everyone else is "so stretched."

It seemed easy for them to believe that if they made me work a Tuesday to cover someone, along with my own days when patients had already booked appointments, I would still be fine since everyone else worked five days a week. It never occurred to them that those days of my life were the ones most planned out, with multiple doctors' appointments, as much as the day could hold.

It would now be a monumental task trying to reschedule three or four different appointments, some of which were bloodwork needed to be able to get more medicine, which might be running out. So now, I was going to have to wait again for another opportunity to do the lab draw, which then meant rescheduling the appointment to review these labs to get my medication. Sometimes it was a critical intention where I was planning on getting some IV fluids that day as a preventive measure against my looming menstrual cycle.

As I stood there trying desperately to explain why I could not be of help to "fill in on Thursday," without going into the tiresome details of my life, I could hear the disappointment in their responses and the sentiments not so silently relayed that I was not committed to helping the team out. If only I could tell them about the truly turbulent nature of my health. I was actually trying to protect the team with any preventive measure I knew, so that I would decrease the odds of randomly crashing and causing an upset in my schedule. If only they could see that they, by simply asking me to compromise that "one silly little day," that they were causing a crazy domino effect that would soon impact the team and cause them to blame me. For the moment, I choose the lesser of the two evils, and I say ever so softly, "I'm so sorry, I hope you know that I would if I could, but I can't."

However, one day, I was tired of saying that I couldn't. Looking back, I probably just wanted them to look at me with feelings of admiration and relief that I would be able to save the day, which is sad because whenever I saved the day, it was never a credit given to me. If anything, it seemed to validate their claim that I was the less busy one, and everyone else still acted as though, for that week anyway, the playing field was leveled, and I would be back to having unfair advantages the following week. However, covering that one day was not without consequence to me.

So, when the thought came to me to cover the extra day for my team, skip my follow-up appointment for medication refills, and write myself a prescription, it seemed like the most ingenious idea that would solve all my problems. After all, I was already on these medications and would be writing for a medication very regularly prescribed for me. This train of thought all seemed logical to me in a bind, but it was the beginning of a slippery slope.

I needed my medications and knew that without them, all systems would crash and my health would be severely compromised. Some of these medications could not be stopped abruptly; they had to be titrated off, and some needed bloodwork to properly monitor how my body was reacting to them. In one case, it would take me two weeks of close medical monitoring to discontinue that medication, so that was out of the equation. I could lose my job for being away that long. At the very least, I would have a whole team of doctors incredibly angry at me for adding to their already full plates. And it would take a long time to get out of the doghouse on that one. Maybe I would lose my job, and most importantly, in my world, my health insurance. That thought always came with a dread that only left after much prayer.

I wish I could tell you just how crazy things became. But I'm sure you have a pretty good idea of what ultimately happened. My two worlds collided in a major way, disappointing so many people, but most importantly, disappointing the God I so love. Thankfully, in the end, the merciful Creator gave me a chance to make things right before any real damage was done.

It has taken a long time to forgive myself. But today, I look back and wish a thousand times that I had fought for myself at my jobs, because as bad as this option to skip my doctor's appointment was, it paled in comparison to what I almost ended up doing. I chose the job over myself and hurt myself badly. I will never again sell myself short like that for anyone or anything! I have come a long way over the years in growing in wisdom and finding out what truly matters and what is negotiable. My health should never have been negotiable. I know better now, and my faith has grown and become too important to me to ever let that happen again.

I chose to share about this here because when you look at a person battling a chronic invisible illness like Sickle Cell disease, please think past your stereotypes of laziness or wanting to come to your emergency rooms for drugs. Just to hold down a job or go to school is an "Olympic" feat, often to an extent you will never know. And sometimes to make all those things work, we may end up pretty much compromising ourselves. Furthermore, the last thing we can afford to do is waste time. As hard as our lives can be, we still try to live it, and still want it to count.

When we decide we can't go any further, it's not because we are lazy. It is because it might end up costing us our health, or maybe our very lives. Going to work or school with active Sickle Cell disease is like trying to juggle full-time jobs while going through active cancer treatment with chemotherapy and radiation. If you think this is an exaggeration, you clearly do not know the extent of impact of this genetic disease. I have lived up close and personal with loved ones going through the exhaustion and pain of advanced cancer. Their journey often sounded like mine as they described it to me.

You often have compassion for people dealing with leukemia who are having a rough time. As inconvenient as it may be, you appeal to your better angels and don't become annoyed when they need to leave early from their jobs for appointments. If they were to walk into an emergency room needing pain medication, you would likely offer them a place to lay their fatigued body down as you try to figure out what might be aggravating their bone marrow this time around. And however long it took them to recuperate, be it two days or two weeks, your kind heart would invest in helping them get better.

I simply wish for this type of care for patients when their misbehaving bone marrow cells are red instead of white.

ALL RISE!

Part 3

CHAPTER 9

PROVING MY DISABILITY

As I sit here writing this, I look through the broad expanse of my sliding doors into the garden outside. It is such a still day that none of the trees or plants or even the vines on the fences are moving. And yet inside of me, there is a storm passing over.

I just received a call to confirm receipt of my application for disability. I tell you it was a grueling process for me. It was not because of the copious amounts of paperwork that needed to be completed, recalling all the names of doctors, past and present, or listing the hospitalizations for which I had lost count. Rather, it was because once again, I was being brought to the carpet to prove that I really have a disability, all while I was refusing to believe it was happening to my body. I mean, seriously!

People would naturally think that someone applying for disability believes they are disabled. The sad truth is that even as I apply for this, I can't believe it's actually real, that my health has declined to the miserable point that I'm unable to predict how functional I will be for the rest of the day even when I wake up feeling decent.

So, as I sit here breathing oxygen out of a nasal cannula, drinking down this "oral chemotherapy medication," and trying to find a comfortable position for my repeatedly replaced hip, I feel so very...confused.

I have heard so many mixed messages along the way about what my health 'should have been like' based on my diagnosis of Sickle Cell SC disease that I have lived in a fair amount of denial myself. If hematologists are going to give me a choice of believing either (a) "You're sickling so much, hence constantly damaging your lungs and are at risk of strokes" OR (b) "Your health should not be too bad, you have Sickle Cell disease 'SC' not 'SS', so your disease course should be relatively milder", which one do you think this hard-working, ambitious black woman is going to pick? Whichever one that lets me stay on the field and play ball with the other players longer, that's definitely the one! I'm a doctor, and I'm not stupid!

I know being tagged with a life-threatening illness is a death sentence for a demanding profession like medicine, where you often sacrifice your health and sleep to take care of others. It's grueling, and not for the faint of heart. So, when doctors are picking who they want on their team, you can be sure they don't want to hear about anything that would leave them playing one man down at any given time. And so, at times like this, I conveniently opted to believe the "specialists" who've told me I "should not be so sick." Problem is, I don't think my blood disorder ever had plans of toeing the line or following the medical books and authorities on how it was "supposed to behave."

So, it was this paradox that often left me hopeful at first and sorrowful by the end of every season of my life. Every year of schooling, every year of training and every job, I would walk in so brave, well and optimistic. But eventually, I would crawl out with my tail between my legs, scratching my head and wondering what went wrong, and when the "mild" part of my illness was going to kick in.

I didn't know too many healthy people who spent their college years in and out of hospitals, studying for finals with a book in one arm and an IV pole with a blood transfusion going in the other. I certainly don't think healthy people have mini-strokes and pulmonary emboli, causing mild heart attacks in their twenties that left them in need of frequent blood transfusions, just to keep these things from recurring. That's all crazy stuff! No one I knew wore portable oxygen or has had multiple hip replacement surgeries by their thirties! That is decidedly not normal! In fact, it sounds terrible, right? And guess what, it is!

No one knew what was wrong with me my entire childhood years. At that time, we lived in a country in South America where access to medical care was quite limited, especially when we were often hurting financially. Whenever I became ill, I was encouraged to jump right back in the game as quickly as possible, getting back to school and life as I knew it. And I did. I remember being very fatigued during these times, more so than the average child based on how active my other friends were. But in isolation, fatigue could be overlooked very easily, especially in a child.

It was not until I was twelve years old and got my first medical evaluation, that my world for the first time crumbled around me. I learned that I should have been closely monitored, because by the time we presented to a hospital, my first ever hospital visit, I was found to be severely anemic and needing blood transfusions. At that time, I could hardly breathe, and they called it pneumonia. It turned out I had my first Acute Chest Syndrome, the leading cause of death in Sickle Cell disease.[1]

After being hospitalized for one month straight, I was finally sent home, feeling quite weak. I had escaped with my life, but still no diagnosis. I had learned that I was severely anemic, but after receiving blood, I was released with no follow-up, nothing to indicate that what I had was a chronic and life-threatening illness. So once again, I stood with my feeble knees and walked back into life as I knew it. And that's what I have been doing ever since.

Everyone thinks that all of Sickle Cell disease is represented by hemoglobin SS and are hardly ever educated that there are other commonly presenting genotypes like SC (mine), S Beta-Thal zero, S Beta-Thal+, and so on. If different therapies are needed for different genotypes, it will take a long time to find out, certainly a much longer time than it has already taken for hemoglobin SS to be studied and treated.

Because most of the research is geared towards studying the behavior of hemoglobin SS and therapies to combat that genotype, I sometimes think it has been an error to lump the other genotypes together with this genotype. Most of those therapies, perfected in people with hemoglobin SS, for the most part, are then doled out to those of us with other genotypes as though it is a done deal that we would respond the same favorable way. Leukemias, or white blood cell disorders of the bone marrow, are in one group. However, each type varies from the next, requiring a different approach and treatment plan. So why we would think one size fits all for our red blood cell disorders of the bone marrow, it's beyond me.

I was told after I was finally diagnosed at age 19 that I should tell my future doctors that "I am hemoglobin SC but I present like hemoglobin SS." Those were my exact marching orders. I was moving to California after being treated at the same hospital for the first three years since my diagnosis (wonderful pediatric team of doctors at Columbia Presbyterian, now called New York Presbyterian).

As I have shared in my first book,[2] my diagnosis had already been a dramatic one, with me being in a coma for several days, and even coding at one point. All this only to wake up and realize that the pains of previous years that I had endured were signaling organ and tissue damage that was never picked up despite my many complaints to the healthcare providers at the student health center at my college and the local hospital emergency room. "Everything is fine," they said. "The tests are normal," they said. And the tests *were* normal, the ones they had at their disposal anyway. But everything had not been fine. Many things were very wrong.

Suddenly, my body was in shambles, and I had collapsed lungs with an infarcted right lower lobe, a spleen that had sickled until it destroyed itself (I felt every moment of that one), fevers that went so high they destroyed my muscles, leaving me unable to walk. I could go on.

But brick by brick I had rebuilt my life over the next three years, with exchange transfusions and hospital stays too many to count all while I finished college. And now, I was heading to California, away from the cold that had taken the life of a friend with Sickle Cell disease the year prior.

In the ignorance of the times, my wonderful doctors (and they truly were) could not understand why I was Sickle Cell SC and "falling apart" like this. They had associated the SC genotype with a milder course of the disease, especially because we have higher hemoglobin levels. They never got that more bad cells could mean serious calamity in other areas. They were just happy that my anemia was "not as severe."

My anemia may not have been as severe, but my disease surely was! And everyone seemed confused by that, so much so that they repeatedly drilled into me that whoever I saw, any doctor of any specialty, I should give them the message, "I am hemoglobin SC, but I present like hemoglobin SS."

To be honest, for years, it made for a very confusing picture because I kept wondering why my body was behaving so much more dramatically than people expected of me. But today I realize that statement was truly inaccurate. I have since met hundreds of people with SC, many of them like me, and many of them not. I have also met many SS patients, many of them like me, some milder, and some worse. And I slowly realized the mistake we had made in Hematology with these genotypes. Instead of appreciating the variance in each, and seeing the challenges unique to each genotype, that each group could have active and deadly disease, we kept wanting to simplify things by lumping them all into one neat little group. But the genotypes do not always "obey!"

I can tell you that nothing irks me more than when a doctor tells me that my hemoglobin is "almost normal." It signals to me that they too are just shuffling along not asking the pertinent questions. It hurts more when it's a hematologist because I figure it's their specialty.

Now, think outside the box. Would more abnormal, sticky cells in my blood vessels be good? Hmmm...Since they are so sticky, wouldn't they just clog more? Would a patient not be at a higher risk of strokes and infarcts and pulmonary emboli when their hemoglobin is "almost normal?" Is it so good to have a "normal level" of *abnormal* cells? Maybe you should be more concerned that I am at a "normal level." That's like telling someone with Polycythemia Vera disorder "great, look how high your hemoglobin level is! It's on the highest end of normal!

From where I sit, I still want to believe I am six feet tall with not a broken bone in my body, and my sky is always blue, and my cup is always half full... But the paperwork I completed says I have had multiple episodes of acute chest syndrome causing pulmonary compromise, and I am now wearing supplemental portable oxygen permanently. It also says I have had five hip surgeries (did I mention all on the same hip?) with placement of a locked-in hip that will give me the limited mobility of an older person and force me to walk with a cane. That same form says I have had surgery in my back with repeated compression fractures and a thoracic cast. BUT I have SC, and it is *supposed to be* mild. So, I'm not sure whose paperwork this is.

References

1. Acute chest syndrome in adults with Sickle Cell disease Authors: Joshua J Field MD, Michael R DeBaun MD, MPH, UpToDate Feb 2019 https://www.uptodate.com/contents/acute-chest-syndrome-in-adults-with-sickle-cell-disease
2. "Awake" chapter 3, p23-27 A Doctor in a Patient's Body: Dreaming Big with Sickle Cell Disease and Chronic Pain Simone Eastman Uwan MD. https://www.amazon.com/dp/1731044267

CHAPTER 10
NOT FOR COMFORT

It is a curious thing that although the equianalgesic dosing chart[1] exists with just a cursory search online, it is so little used in the management of pain in a Sickle Cell patient.

Today, I had to explain to a hesitant nurse that it was worth paging the attending assigned to my case for two reasons. The first reason is that he should not have taken away the oral pain medications that I normally use around the clock at home to cover my baseline pain. If he does this, he will never know when my acute pain in the hospital has decreased, and I have returned to my baseline. He will not know that I can now be managed with my home medications if he never included them with the inpatient regimen, to begin with.

Furthermore, he removed my home medications to cover me with IV pain therapy but chose a pain protocol with a dosage equivalent much less than my oral pain pills! So now, I left my home where my oral pain pills were poorly managing this Sickle Cell crisis and agreed to be hospitalized, hoping to manage my pain. But it seems that instead I will be holding my head and grinding my teeth and begging the entire medical staff one after another, appearing to be "drug-seeking" because in essence, I now have *less* medication to help me after coming to the hospital. And all because they did not bother to calculate the equianalgesic dosage going from my oral pain medications they removed to the IV pain therapy protocol they have now put in its place.

Okay, so let's review the dosing. Based on the equianalgesic dosing chart, 1mg of IV morphine is equivalent to 3mg of oral morphine.

Let's say I take 30 mg of oral morphine daily, that is, 10mg of IV in a 24-hr period. If you write 1mg q4hrs, that is only 6mg IV in 24 hours, not the 10mg that would match my home regimen. So, in placing my life in your hands, you have jeopardized it. The Hippocratic oath of "first do no harm" has already been effortlessly violated. You have harmed me by decreasing my medication, unmasking and unleashing torrents of pain and causing physiological stress all while I'm in an active and worsening Sickle Cell crisis. FANTASTIC!

I'm finally greeted by my nurse again and get a chance to ask her, "so, for what reason do you believe pain medications are given to patients?" And I receive the predictable, usually incomplete answer "To make them comfortable." Now, I see why a nurse would take their sweet time coming to give me my pain pills if they thought it was only for the patient's comfort.

I had asked the nurse for my scheduled pain pills almost an hour ago, and no one was currently in sight. When the nurse's assistant came, he looked at the time upon my second request for pain medication. Seeing 6:45 pm, he proceeded to tell me that since the nurses were about to do their end of shift huddle at 7:00 pm, I would have to wait until the shift change rounds were over and I would get my pills then.

He said it so causally you would have believed that I had asked for a piece of chewing gum! Mind you, at the time I had asked the nurse for my pain medication, it was already past due, and my pain had crept up to a 7/10 while I slept. And these were scheduled medications!

When the nurse finally came, she answered my question, saying that the pain medications are to make people comfortable. I pointed out to her that the health industry would usually not be that preoccupied just with making people comfortable.

It was not ONLY for comfort that pain was established to be the fifth vital sign by the Joint Commission in 2001 when assessing a patient.[2] Pain can trigger a response that can ultimately harm the body during a Sickle Cell crisis. That is why pain needs to be evaluated and treated promptly.

When someone experiences pain, their body experiences stress. This kind of fight or flight stress produces cortisol, which suppresses the immune system, tenses up the body and can even cause a person to splint when breathing, not allowing proper oxygenation of tissue.[3] All these things would harm the body further, versus helping it heal.

It is the very reason that someone undergoing surgery is put to sleep and anesthetized. The pain they would feel otherwise would simply be unbearable. People are not offered the option of surgery without anesthesia because it is understood that this level of pain, if felt while conscious or without anesthesia for pain management, would send a person's body into shock, leading to heart failure and quite possibly death.

Now imagine a Sickle Cell patient waiting in the emergency room for hours with such a painful condition, as neurotransmitters containing stress molecules of every kind get released in generous amounts in the body. As pain mounts, and it becomes difficult to breathe causing poor oxygenation, even more cells sickle and block blood vessels. This leads to more vaso-occlusion and death of organs and tissues. Death! It is an occurrence that cannot be repaired or reversed in many parts of the body. Simply because someone thought there was no rush to make us "comfortable" and went to do something else instead. Each time that we providers allow this to happen, we are essentially saying, "everyone else needs to be put to sleep and anesthetized for surgery. But you, you Sickle Cell patient, you will be having your surgery while you are wide awake, and you will not be receiving any anesthesia. And since we don't consider your situation urgent, it will be okay if we go and attend to other things during your surgery. We will return... eventually."

Think about that the next time you see someone with Sickle Cell disease waiting more than twenty minutes in the "emergency" room. Think about it the next patient you have in the hospital who is crying while it is not yet time for medication, and there are two more hours to go. Think about it when you choose to attend to something else instead of giving a scheduled or requested pain medication. Because really and truly, it is NOT just for comfort.

References

1. "Opiate Equianalgesic Dosing Chart" UNC Health Care Guideline University of North Carolina Hospitals, December 2009 https://www.med.unc.edu/aging/files/2018/06/Analgesic-Equivalent-Chart.pdf
2. "Pain as the 5th Vital Sign: Exposing the Vital Need For Pain Education" Natalia E. Morone, MD, MS and Debra K. Weiner, MD Clin Ther. 2013 Nov; 35(11): 1728–1732. https://www.ncbi.nlm.nih.gov/pmc/articles/PMC3888154/
3. "Understanding the stress response: Chronic activation of this survival mechanism impairs health" Harvard Health Publishing, Harvard Medical School, March 2011 https://www.health.harvard.edu/staying-healthy/understanding-the-stress-response

CHAPTER 11

WHY DON'T YOU BELIEVE ME? (SPOKEN WORD)

Have you met me before? I could have sworn by the way you were looking at me, by the way your smile never reaches your eyes, that you had met me before, and I had done you wrong. You would think I knew the rules of the game, but I was somehow still violating them, just to make you lose your cool. Something is very wrong with the way you are speaking to me, as though you caught me with my hand in your cookie jar, and you had video-taped evidence to prove me a thief, as you say to me "You're not in a Sickle Cell crisis. Your 'crit' is normal!"

The nonverbal communication between your colleagues is not missed either. There seems to be an unspoken consensus that I am not to be believed.

You agree that my blood pressure is unusually high, completely normalizing with a dose of Dilaudid. And you agree that my electrophoresis results, which I brought with me have corroborated my "story" of Sickle Cell disease.

I prepared you, explaining that I sometimes have normal hemoglobin levels during my crises. I told you of my lung infarcts only showing up on imaging two weeks after the incident, only when healing had started and calcification now highlighted its margins. Yet you have still chosen to render medical treatment only to your textbooks.

I don't know how to tell you this, but your textbooks are inaccurate. Oh, they have what you know so far, but surprisingly, that's very little!

I know what's going wrong, but you won't listen to me. You are nervous to admit my pain because this obligates you to do something about it. And how can you, when the medicines you have, those same medicines others overdose on, I drink like water through my veins and still cry out in 10 out of 10 pain.

Yet, you probably lost a patient today because of overdose. I know what's wrong, but you won't believe me because your big impressive medical books have not caught up yet. They tell you that Sickle Cell disease is a hemoglobinopathy that is homozygous recessive, with marked anemia, with a hematocrit that falls to the floor in a Sickle Cell crisis, and with an obvious reticulocyte count, plus or minus a leukocytosis and other associated symptoms.

They forgot to include that there are dozens of hemoglobinopathies that become complicated once saddled with just one sickle gene. We are not all homozygous recessive but double heterozygous, with two mismatched alleles, both very abnormal that meet and cause their net effect to be greater than the sum of their parts. There is SC, the one you often say is "not as bad" because it has a "less severe anemia." But a less severe anemia does not mean a less severe illness. It's just a different presentation.

90

Have you stopped to think that this person with "more blood" has a larger quantity of abnormal cells, increasing the viscosity and likelihood of blockage? And there you have it doctors and nurses, your increased incidence of a vaso-occlusive crises; the ones you will hardly recognize because you say "your 'crit is normal" and force me out as though I ever wanted to be with you. I'm missing the concert with tickets that cost me a small fortune! Yes, there may be less anemia, but my extra abnormal cells that make my hematocrit look normal, have now put me at risk of a stroke, or a pulmonary embolus, maybe Avascular Necrosis, but all with certain end-organ damage. Turns out those invisible acute onset pain signals still mean danger, even as you look only for signs but ignore my symptoms and send me home undertreated, or perhaps not treated at all. I hope I don't become ineligible for a stem cell transplant, or a promising clinical trial. I pray I'm not too sick for the pound of cure because you held back "an ounce of prevention" each time I'm presented with only symptoms to explain my internal torture.

And there are many more patients being treated like me; the S Beta-thalassemia zero, S Beta-thalassemia plus, SO Arab, SE, SD, all with a range of presentations, all of which can present with hemolytic anemia at times and look like the typical low hematocrit SS, or can unfortunately present with early vaso-occlusive crisis, and completely normal blood results, as least as far as a CBC with a differential goes. One day you will develop a test that will vindicate me. I hope I'm around to see it.

I understand. This is not yet in your books. I know. I've seen your medical books. The irony is that whoever contributed that partial information you now use like the whole law, were likely compassionate researchers wanting some truth to be known so that we "sicklers" could get help.

But they, even with best of intentions, are studying a house from the outside. They are limited in what they can see. They may peep through the windows and bend around the doors, but their vantage point will always be limited.

Now I, your present "sickler," live in that house. I know every room and can tell you about it, in your language if you choose. I know medicalese! I trained with the best of you! I'm a Stanford University School of Medicine graduate. And just so you know, Harvard wanted me too, but it was just too frosty that way. I don't do cold weather well. I went to the "Harvard of the West Coast" instead. And while I was there, I learned your language.

But even if I did not, you know the universal language of the human race; a common tongue. You could have at least listened to the dozens of people you see who do not speak medicalese but actually live in that Sickle Cell "house." Their stories are so similar, yet few in Healthcare are listening.

So, for now, I will be sent home. Though my laboratory results may change in a week or so, and vindicate me only after the fact, your shift will be long over by then, with your mind made up that I was... "acting." I will never receive the benefit of your doubt because you are determined to treat your textbooks, and still send me the medical bill. What an expensive waste of my time. I just wish you could believe me.

CHAPTER 12

PTSD

Have you ever been hurt, as a child or an adult, and decided to find an authority-figure to let them know, with great emphasis, that you are hurt? Have you ever, after going into great detail about someone or something hurting you, had that same authority-figure, instead of embracing you and protecting you, and telling you that everything would be OK, turn around and tell you that you were lying?

Have you had someone yell at you to shut up, insisting that you were making something up when in your heart, you knew it was as real as the ground on which you were standing? And maybe, depending on how old you were, they ordered you to leave - leave your home, leave the job, leave your place of security-just get lost.

What did you do after that? You likely acquired a learned helplessness, deciding you could only trust and depend on yourself. And since you were in no position to fight, or change the situation, you grew a thick skin to cover the gaping wound of betrayal and just moved on. Maybe you even decided never to trust that type of authority again. With time, it was likely reinforced that what you had to say on "that particular issue" was a topic no one wanted to hear. They could not handle it. Telling them would require a response on their part to fix the situation. But whatever that response was might cause great upheaval for those involved if anyone chose to fight for you. The only other option they saw then, was to pretend your story did not happen, or it was not happening. So, they did just that.

You could only find solace in other people who had the same hurt. There, you could cry and tell the truth and let down your guard. You find yourself recalling your traumatic event, repeatedly, yet the feeling of abandonment and upset does not leave. Someone recommends that you see a psychiatrist, and your psychiatrist gave it a name - post-traumatic stress disorder (PTSD).

Many of your Sickle Cell patients are walking around with PTSD. Let me show you how, and why.

GROWING UP

For many of us, it started when we were young and were confronted with a diagnosis of what seemed to be the perfect torture. Firstly, it was invisible. Except for the test that provided the diagnosis, there was not much to show. There was a pain that could hit at any moment and accelerate from zero to "God help me" in about 15 minutes flat. Sometimes it left as suddenly as it came, but often, it ballooned into full-on internal torture that you could barely describe to your family members.

It could range from two hours to two weeks, or sadly though not as often, two whole months. And while the war was raging in your body and attacking all systems -wherever blood flows - you were burdened with the task of convincing your family, friends, and schoolmates that this was a legitimate manifestation even though they saw nothing. It was your private torture.

Heaven forbid that it was your turn to wash the dishes or assume some other responsibility at home or school because then, you were faced with having to prove you did not conspire with the universe to get sick on purpose. While some just gave a helping hand to a person in need, others made sure you knew what an inconvenience you were. Without a doubt, there was sadness, loneliness, and stress with each episode.

Eventually, you knew the Sickle Cell symptoms all too well, that short period before the onset of a crisis. It is almost like an aura, a forewarning. The time varied greatly between warning and onset of a Sickle Cell crisis, but when you felt that aura, panic would set in. "No, no, no, please don't come, I have exams!" "Please, don't come. I have to attend my friend's party." "Please, it's my turn to do 'xyz' and they are going to be so angry with me if I can't do it. PLEASE!"

Over the years, those outcries became, "Nooo! Don't make me miss my own graduation!". Or, "Nooo, I paid a lot for that cruise!" Even more impactful, "I really liked that guy. Why did I have to get sick for so long? And since I *look* so well, he probably thinks I did this on purpose, or maybe it's not as painful as I claim. Who could blame him for walking away, with this disease that exacts its damage where no one can see? I probably looked like a drama queen yelling and carrying on. Oh well..."

That cycle continues right into adulthood as you watch your support systems wane, watch potential suitors walk away, and wonder if the next episode will end your life. It is no wonder that anxiety and depression become prevalent.

PTSD- HEALTHCARE INDUCED

According to the National Institutes of Health (NIH), Institute of Mental Health, post-traumatic stress disorder, or PTSD is a disorder that develops in some people who have experienced a shocking, scary or dangerous event".[1]

This, as we will soon see, can easily describe people as they navigate the emergency room during a Sickle Cell crisis.

Mayo Clinic says, "PTSD is a mental health condition that is triggered by a terrifying event- either experiencing it or witnessing it".[2]

Based on this description, PTSD can now be extended to our caregivers, since they often experience the emergency room with us, and are witnesses of what we go through. Many times, when we present to the ER, healthcare providers are not familiar with our disease, and so in the middle of a Sickle Cell crisis, we are having to educate them about the disease at the time that we are crashing.

I have a friend, Jenny who would come with me whenever I presented to the emergency room for care. On one occasion, they were trying to access a vein, and I was stuck thirteen times before ultimately having an intra-jugular central line placed in my neck. By the time she saw the thirteenth stick, she broke down and with tears in her eyes said, "this is horrible, I can't believe this is what you go through."

Meanwhile, I had been consoling each nurse who failed to access my veins, apologizing for being a hard stick. They were all so wonderful that day, and each nurse would express sympathy after failing to access my overprotective veins.

For me, such a day was just considered another crazy day in my life. But my central line, which looked for all intents and purposes like tubing sewn into my jugular vein and hanging off the side of my neck, was of no comfort to my friend or my husband who came to be with me later. Witnessing all that happened had been traumatic for them. We often think only of the patient and the toll the disease takes on them. But watching your loved one suffer, and not being able to do anything about it, can be quite painful emotionally. Caregiver stress is real!

But how does PTSD happen in the healthcare setting? Here is how. A Sickle cell patient experiences a physical trauma called a Sickle Cell crisis. When this happens, we will usually present and report this trauma to a doctor or nurse. When we present, in the case of the urgent care or emergency room setting, we may encounter a physician who is well familiar with Sickle Cell disease, which almost immediately relieves our panic and decreases the "fight or flight" response[3] that was triggered at the thought of possibly encountering a doctor who is a novice to our disorder.

Unfortunately, we are more likely to experience a doctor who is ignorant of the management of Sickle Cell, or worse, indifferent to the implications of the suffering. We get one of two responses. The first response is "your blood and imaging results were normal! We have no reason to admit you. Go home and follow up with your primary care physician. This is usually all while we are experiencing eight to ten out of ten pain- only that level brings us to the emergency room.

We have no way of treating this type of pain at home. The doctor has not read the 2014 guidelines for Sickle Cell management which discusses that a patient with Sickle Cell crisis can present with normal laboratory results and that there is still no bloodwork that can reflect a Sickle Cell crisis with high accuracy. [4] Many of them are not even aware that these helpful parameters exist, including things like how to manage acute pain in a Sickle Cell patient presenting in a crisis. These instructions were created by the NIH for both outpatient and inpatient care, and they cover treatment for just about every system of the body, for problems that affect Sickle Cell patients.[5] However, since they are considered guidelines (suggestions, or at best experienced advice) instead of protocols, (procedures that are required or mandatory), doctors are not held accountable if they ignore the input, and patients receive poor care.

Meanwhile, our motives are questioned for why we even presented to the emergency room, and no significant treatment is given. We are disappointed. We stretched out our hands and allowed them to poke and prod us while we were very sick. And now, we are made to feel like we made up the whole thing. We shut down emotionally. The questions become "who can we turn to for help? Who can we trust?" This is an extremely vulnerable time for the Sickle Cell patient because it is possible that we might seek help or pain meds from other sources that might not be safe.

I know of a case in Los Angeles of a woman with Sickle Cell disease who was charged with 17 counts of possession of marijuana, with five of them being felony counts.[6,7] She was ultimately exonerated of all counts because she was able to show records of being repeatedly turned away from the emergency room without adequate pain medication even though she presented each time with moderate to severe pain, documented clearly in her Emergency medical records at initial presentation. She was likely a patient with normal-appearing labs.

The second response that we may get is more welcoming, at least initially. "All your results are abnormal, your hemoglobin is low, your reticulocyte count is high, and you have a leukocytosis." At this news, the patient usually says a silent hallelujah that this time around, the chaos in his or her blood has revealed itself and vindicated them. We will be allowed to get some relief and treatment for any underlying problems. Today, we get to focus on just getting better.

But that relief is short-lived. We get admitted, and we are placed on a protocol that falls far below our actual need for pain control. We may be placed on the typical existing pain protocol the hospital has. We may be given this for treatment of our advanced pain, when in fact, we are veterans to many of the medications and have developed significant tolerances to them. Now we need a higher dosage than when we first started using these medications to accomplish the same desired result. Many times, the dosage we receive is just barely more than what we are already using at home.

It does not take long before our motives are questioned for the amount or frequency of medication that we are needing to ease our pain, even as our systems are obviously falling apart, based on every imaging, laboratory results, or other measurable data. Though it may be obvious that we are sick, we do not have the luxury of laying in peace and healing. We must now worry about the quality of care we will receive. We must articulate clearly, hoping that someone will find us worthy of being listened to and having proper treatment, so that we make it out of that admission alive.

There is a stain on the collective consciences of everyone in the healthcare industry, because many patients, even with measurable abnormalities, are pushed out or discharged prematurely simply because the medical staff has become frustrated with treating us. In our case, many doctors have not been trained in the management of continuous pain, comparable to end-stage cancer pain,[8,9] but ongoing as in the case of Sickle Cell. Because of this, they become uncomfortable having the patient around. Doctors like to feel in control, and when they don't, they want the source of their problem to disappear.

I have been on the other side of this equation and can attest to these things happening. Even pharmacists will complain to the doctors and nurses that they are not comfortable with the amount of pain medication being dispensed. Often, they will ask the staff to do whatever can be done to help the patient be discharged. It is at this point that I have seen nurses become disagreeable toward a patient entrusted to their care, in response to these directives. They often feel for the patient, but feel helpless and caught in the middle, which results in a frustration that is transferred to the patient. They will distance themselves and hardly respond if they are paged to the patient's room.

And we, the patients, observe the sudden shift in attitude. We sense something has happened. And we feel abandoned. We are subsequently told we will be discharged while we are not yet stable, and still in considerable pain. You will hear of these experiences from thousands of patients and caregivers across the country. We do not know each other, but our stories are almost identical.

To be fair, I believe that part of the problem is also the fear of overdosing a patient. While for many of these narcotic analgesics, it is said that there is no ceiling-effect, doctors are scared. They have probably had patients who died of overdose with these same medications. Yet, here we are, the Sickle Cell patients, being infused with relatively large amounts of potent medications, and often not relieved of our pains much at all! These drugs are often no match for our pain, unyielding to the best they have to offer. In this setting, their fears and prejudices become unveiled.

Yet, there seems to be no worthy "competitor" to the narcotic analgesic, something that would rival their efficacy in pain control, in an oral or intravenous preparation. As a result, we patients are sent home under-treated, left to fend for ourselves. This puts us at risk for utilizing other possibly unsafe things to get relief.

When the crisis finally subsides, and our lives are a little calmer, we reflect on the emergency room/hospital experience and often will feel like we were disrespected, distrusted and demeaned by healthcare providers, all while we were down. Patients will then think that doctors, the pharmaceutical industry, the research community, etc. cannot be trusted. Some patients may not know where one field of medicine ends, and another begins. So, the entire medical establishment is painted with a broad brush.

The thought toward hospital providers becomes "if they are repeatedly sending me home in pain and as unstable as I am, then they could not possibly care about me. Therefore, I cannot trust them." It becomes a simple "if-then" conditional equation.

Whenever we think of returning to the emergency room, it produces extreme anxiety which in turn can cause 'fight-or-flight' stress response-rapid heartbeat, tense muscles, shallow breathing,[3] which only makes things worse and can even trigger a crisis. We, patients, may feel like we left the hospital or ER with a bigger wound than the one we went to treat. We may have been helped physically, but the emotional wound that was inflicted on us was worse. In the long run, that sore often creates a bigger and more enduring problem than the crisis we came with.

When the thought of having to ever return to the emergency room produces anxiety from fear of a repeat of a previous encounter, that is post-traumatic stress disorder (PTSD). When you are stuck on the experiences of being mistreated, and it produces a negative physical response in your body each time you think about, it is PTSD. When you pull away from family and friends, and you can only talk about these things in a support group setting because you feel unsafe, like nobody cares and the only person that could understand is another Sickle Cell patient, that becomes PTSD. That is post-traumatic stress from an event that was significant enough to make someone decide that they so hated going to the emergency room, they so hated their dignity being taken away, that they would rather stay home and suffer, knowing they could die for doing so.

Why does it matter? We will examine the consequences, and unfortunate effects on the healthcare system if these things are not addressed.

References

1. "Post-Traumatic Stress Disorder" NIH, National Institute of Mental Health, May 2019 https://www.nimh.nih.gov/health/topics/post-traumatic-stress-disorder-ptsd/index.shtml
2. "Post-traumatic stress disorder (PTSD)," Mayo Clinic July 2018 https://www.mayoclinic.org/diseases-conditions/post-traumatic-stress disorder/symptoms-causes/syc-20355967
3. Understanding the stress response: Chronic activation of this survival mechanism impairs health" Harvard Health Publishing, Harvard Medical School, March 2011 https://www.health.harvard.edu/staying-healthy/understanding-the-stress-response
4. "Managing Acute Complications of Sickle Cell Disease" ,Evidence Based Management of Sickle Cell Disease Expert Panel 2014, Chapter 3, p31 https://www.nhlbi.nih.gov/sites/default/files/media/docs/sickle-cell-disease
5. "Managing Acute Complications of Sickle Cell Disease" ,Evidence Based Management of Sickle Cell Disease Expert Panel 2014 https://www.nhlbi.nih.gov/sites/default/files/media/docs/sickle-cell-disease
6. Gorman, Peter. "SISTER SOMAYAH KAMBUI: Burning the Bush for Sickle Cell." Hightimes.com. High Times, 17 Dec. 2002.
7. California NORML. LA Jury Acquits Sister Somayah of Medical Marijuana Charge. CANORML.org. California National Organization for the Reform of Marijuana Laws, 18 Mar. 2002. <http://www.canorml.org/news/somayahacquitted.html>.

8. Treating Sickle Cell pain like cancer pain. Brookoff D, et al. Ann Intern Med. 1992. https://www.ncbi.nlm.nih.gov/m/pubmed/1736768/

9. Sickle Cell Disease: An Opportunity for Palliative Care across the Life Span Diana J. Wilkie, PhD, RN, FAAN et al. The Nursing Clinics of North America, 2010 https://www.ncbi.nlm.nih.gov/pmc/articles/PMC2932707/

CHAPTER 13

REJECTING YOUR CREATION

You have been giving a child morphine since he was two years old. He is now thirty, and the natural opioid response of the brain has been suppressed to the point of extinction. And now your once upon a time two-year-old needs a long-acting medication each day, and when he is admitted, his pain is difficult to treat.

In frustration, you call your ex-baby boy some of the worst names. You don't like him anymore and consider him a monster for coming in to treat his pain crisis and for having the nerve to be needing THAT much medication to palliate his pain.

He on the other hand, has realized that to stay at home with prolonged acute on chronic pain would be to damage his organs, and put himself on the surest path to death from heart failure caused by the stress on a body dealing with pain so out of this world that it has this kind man (normally), this once upon a time two year old baby, cussing and yelling at anyone and everyone to make it stop because the pain is THAT bad.

So, he shows up and takes the insults, because he does not want to die, and he is too weak to defend himself against your anger, frustration, and name-calling under your breath. When he is better, he is sad and angry that you belittled and insulted him when he did the only thing he knew to do. He becomes hostile from the hurt, and the next happy unsuspecting nurse gets the brunt of it — a vicious cycle.

I heard a man with Sickle Cell disease share about a doctor who convinced him that he was a drug addict for treating his Sickle Cell disease with "that much" pain medication. And even though he could not agree, his respect for the older doctor made him relent in his defense. He decided to invest a significant sum of money to face his so-called addiction in a drug rehab facility. He gave it his all and went through the program, graduating with distinction and feeling very proud that he could accomplish this goal of having absolutely no pain medication in his system.

Only days after graduating from the expensive program, the poor fellow had a whopping Sickle Cell crisis and was rushed to the hospital. They were about to load him with IV narcotics to stop the pain when he wailed that he had spent thousands of dollars to overcome his "addiction," so please can he have something else, anything else, for his overwhelming pain.

The response he received was the saddest of all. "We don't have anything else for this level of pain. I'm afraid narcotic analgesic is your only option. Which narcotic works best for you?" To address his disappointment and obvious remorse for wasting his money, the kind emergency room doctor that day took the time to explain to him that he never actually had an addiction but an increased tolerance to the medications and maybe dependence. This was not surprising for his chronic painful illness. He had been on this class of drugs since he was two years old. And he had suffered through many Sickle Cell crises so intense that it required more and more pain medication. So, it was no wonder that what started at two years old with morphine had become a difficult to control disease requiring OxyContin and immediate release morphine.

Dear Healthcare providers, please don't put the blame where it does not belong. You were the ones with the keys to the medicine cabinet. We simply asked your thoughts on how best to manage our pain. You created this baby, and now you stand back to curse your creation when you don't even have a decent alternative to give to your once upon a time two-year-old?

He doesn't score drugs on the street for cheap, although it would be so much easier! He comes to you because he does not want to get high but get well. Yet you offer him narcotics with one hand, and spank him for taking it with the other?

Then you send him a bill with costs so staggering, he probably wishes he could have been helped by those street drugs. They are WAY more affordable! He can hardly pay off all the bills sent to him-from you, from the X-ray tech and the EKG tech and the hospital, and from everyone who touched him. And when the bills add up, and he can't pay on time or pay enough, this will affect his credit score, and his ability to buy a home or even a car. If he was only wanting drugs, a stash for a few dollars might have seemed of lesser consequence.

But he is simply seeking the best legitimate help he knows for his aching body and non-compliant bone marrow. So, he bypasses the street dealers and presents to the more expensive emergency room. He endures the long waits that make his pain increase and cause him to lose his mind. And he listens when you enter his room to share your treatment plan knowing full well that your pain protocol will start far below what his pain needs require, and likely you have never laid eyes on the Sickle Cell guidelines for pain management.[1]

When he is discharged, he would not have been referred to a nutritionist for a feasible prevention plan, considering that diet can lessen his symptoms. He needs a diet consult and counseling very much like the diabetic patient, but he won't get that.

Stop it! Just stop it. You have made a wrong assumption, and by now I think you know it. End the madness!

Reference

"Managing Acute Complications of Sickle Cell Disease," Evidence Based Management of Sickle Cell Disease Expert Panel 2014 https://www.nhlbi.nih.gov/sites/default/files/media/docs/sickle-cell-disease

CHAPTER 14

NOT DRUGGED, BUT SEDATED

Dilaudid is a funny medication. Like I tell people, for every point of pain relief you experience, you will be whipped with *three* points of sedation. You will feel an initial sense of relief of your pain, because it does relieve the pain! But it will be followed immediately by a slap of heavy sedation that almost wants to knock you out like Mike Tyson. The happiness from the quick reduction of your pain is barely acknowledged as you fade into rapid sedation. And if you want more pain ease, well, you are getting another *triple* helping of that sedation.

So, you are left in a quagmire. You fight through the sedation to quickly let your care team(nurses and doctors usually) know that while you may not be able to communicate with them through your somnolence, you are also *still* experiencing affliction, especially since that initial pain relief is fading quickly and was never enough in the first place. You manage to convince them to give you one more milligram (one point) of Dilaudid. But along with that, you received three invisible points of sedation. So, out you go again. Your pain relief was never able to rise in equal status to your sedation, and now you are drowning while trying to communicate that.

Someone ignorant of this drug's dosing relationship looking at you, asking for more pain relief while you could barely slur your words to say this, would erroneously think that you are enjoying a drug high. They will likely never consider that maybe you are a rapid metabolizer of the drug you are being given to treat your pain, and the analgesic leaves your system faster than the sedative. Conversely, you may metabolize too slowly, and perhaps only a small amount of the active ingredient from the drug may be available to you, much less than was given to you. They would never know that you were still in great pain. But you are!

As I shared in my first book, this sadly has happened with many nurses, doctors, and pharmacists on a patient's care team. I once had to interject in a conversation I heard between a nurse and the pharmacist verifying patients' medications on the floor. The nurse complained, "you know what makes me mad? When I see the patient's head bobbing, and they are almost passed out from the pain medicine, and yet they're still asking for more! Now tell me that is not drug-seeking behavior!"

Therein lies the problem. I spelled out the difference between analgesia and sedation to them, pointing out that they were in fact looking at sedation. I further explained that the patient could still be in pain because her need for analgesia or pain relief likely had not yet been met. The pharmacist (yes, you heard me correctly) thanked me for pointing this relationship out to her and said she had never considered narcotic analgesics like Dilaudid in this way before. She concluded by telling me that she will never look at Sickle Cell patients in the same way again.

ALL RISE!

Sometimes you cannot fully understand what people are experiencing until you have walked in their shoes. Now, hear me clearly when I say that I do NOT recommend trying any of these medications just for understanding! Just please remember that sometimes you may not have the full picture. You may never have the complete story, so please err on the side of compassion.

ALL RISE!

Part 4

CHAPTER 15

THERE WILL BE CONSEQUENCES

With all that you have heard, I am hoping that you, as an individual (it starts with one), will agree with me that a lot of education and change needs to happen in the management of Sickle Cell disease as a pathology and in the care of the person behind the disease. That person, we must first agree, is worth saving. We must also agree that what we are doing may not be working well and that we need to improve outcomes.

You are dealing with a population of wonderful, intelligent, and compassionate people, and you hardly know us. If you are an outpatient provider you likely see us in increments of 15minutes, often because we are sick and needing care. You do not see us at our best. If you are a hospitalist, you see us maybe a few times a year, for slightly longer periods during a hospital stay. But still, you interact very little. You hardly ask questions that can help you learn. Maybe you think you don't have anything to learn from us. But, like everyone else you meet, we have full lives beyond the walls of your clinic or hospital. What you see, each time we present sick to your clinic, it's likely the worst version of us. We come in vulnerable and broken, but we live beautiful, rich and colorful lives in the world and we have families and friends who see our worth, grieve when we are hurt, and miss us when we are not around.

We are doctors and nurses too, as many of us have the incentive to pursue and create a better way of caring for patients, providing better and more compassionate treatment than what we were shown. We are lawyers and know what to do when HIPPA violations occur, or when there is widespread mismanagement that needs to be reported. We are journalists who know how to spread news through electronic, print, and social media to shine a light on wrongs done to a community and praise the works of the good Samaritans. I know of some wonderful doctors and nurses doing excellent work caring for Sickle Cell patients. This is because their names are acknowledged in a "shout out" for superior care, and it is usually done by patients. These online applauses are usually in our closed groups (closed to the public) with thousands of members, so that others can see which doctors are supporters of patients like us. I say a silent prayer of blessing and well wishes for the name of each provider I see.

Why does it matter? What do we stand to lose if we do not change? More than you realize! It may not be readily apparent, but this is why I have chosen to come forward and write this book. The consequences of doing nothing will affect both parties. Some consequences may be small but significant. The Sickle Cell patient, traumatized by previous experiences, and without any therapy for that trauma, now presents to the emergency room like a cat with an arched back ready for a fight. The next healthcare professional that patient encounters who displays ANY sign of ignorance of the disease or worse, indifference towards it, may be met with the brunt of that patient's unresolved anger despite the provider's overall intention and a possible desire to help.

Regardless of that doctor's attempt at a professional demeanor, I can vouch for most doctors that a negative encounter like this will often frame the way they think about that patient going forward. Then, unfortunately because we tend to generalize, it will extend to thinking that this encounter is typical of all Sickle Cell patients. Bad news spreads faster, so even three "great behaving" Sickle Cell patients often cannot compensate for the unfortunate encounter with one patient. Any further introductions to other "disagreeable" patients perpetuate the idea of Sickle Cell patients being difficult. And all because of displaced anger, frustration and disappointment a patient has, especially towards urgent/emergent care providers for the emotional baggage that we have experienced. It is a vicious cycle. Someone should decide to be more mature and end it.

I am doing the best I can to encourage my Sickle Cell community, despite feeling like they have been hurt so many times by the medical establishment, to still consider terms of peace and what that would look like. It will likely take some self-refection. But since this book is written to those of you in healthcare, I want you to ask yourself if, as a provider, you are part of the problem or the solution when it comes to having positive encounters with Sickle Cell Patients. Are you partaking in conversations that quickly spread a negative stereotype?

It may start from the very moment that you hear that you will be having a Sickle Cell patient in your caseload. I have had my nurse friends tell me of all the eye-rolling, and body language displayed, and even openly demeaning words some providers respond with when they hear that they are receiving a Sickle Cell patient. Are you a part of *that* problem?

Truthfully, anyone can join the herd mentality and act in the same old way. Or, you can choose to grow a little each time that you counter your peers with a more mature perspective. Maybe I can appeal to your highest angel and ask that you remind your colleagues that patients are people at their worst, and some of what the staff is seeing may have a mental health component from recurrent trauma a patient can experience (PTSD). I am not asking you to make continuous excuses for bad behavior, but simply provide insight as to where it is coming from. It's the equivalent of saying, "It's not right. But I understand. The patient still needs to be respectful in any situation, but I get how they got here."

Not every disease or disorder is physically painful to the extent of Sickle Cell disease, with pain that has been compared to end-stage cancer pain. Not every disease requires such frequent interaction with hospitals and emergency rooms. Not every patient walks in, thinking they might not make it almost every time they present to the emergency room. Not everyone walks in knowing how critical they are health-wise and knowing that they need every health-care provider to stop dragging and do something, anything, and quickly, so they don't end up with end-organ damage from late intervention of fluids, oxygen, and delayed pain control. So, please try to walk a little in the shoes of the patient before spewing brainwashed words around like "drug-seeking." Let me clarify that, we ARE drug-seeking!!! We are seeking any medication you have that will shut down the *pain, which reflects the destruction* that is going on in our tissues, bones, and organs. Frankly, you would be drug seeking too in this situation.

When you get the patients who can interact easily while advocating for their medical needs despite their pain, don't forget to point them out to your colleagues and balance the messages they hear, because thankfully, these patients are more in number! They just don't make it into the news of the shift.

Lastly, you might even want to dialog with the patient when their pain is under better control and remind them that despite what they may be thinking, you really are on their side. Just make sure that you mean it.

For those of you that I'm not able to convince to change unhealthy patient relations, I will ask you to consider what I'm about to say next. A few years ago, I read a story about the police department terminating some officers of high rank in their department found to be part of the KKK,[1] here in Florida. The deparment was tipped off because someone sent a photo of one of the men at a KKK meeting, dressed in his garb but without his hood and exposing his face.

I thought long and hard about that story. Based on the information provided, it became obvious that someone he knew turned him in. I say this because as we air our frustrations, intolerances and maybe even prejudices, we have no idea who is listening with disapproval. Maybe it's someone with a heart for justice or worse someone who wants your position or wants you gone and knows how they could use your verbiage to achieve that. Whatever the case may be, consider these things in the workplace.

The person of color you may think likely to report you may be the least likely to do so for many reasons. It may well be someone who appeared to have agreed with you and even said some overtly unsavory things themselves (maybe to cover their tracks) that may expose or report you. With recording devices fitting into pockets, and cameras on phones, it would behoove you to be on your best behavior especially when it comes to mistreatment of patients, like those of us with Sickle Cell disease.

The medical institution has not caught up to the fact that even patients have found ways to expose unprofessional behavior. They have tried the proper channels of reporting misconduct and found them to be ineffective. People are now taking their cases to the court of public opinion since the normal channels are not working for them. Many of you would be surprised to know that you may have been recorded or videotaped, but there are many clips of videos and audio recordings reflecting poor behavior in our healthcare providers across the country. These videos are being shared very liberally across social media in many of the closed groups... It would only be a matter of time that they fall into the hands of professionals who could unfortunately do career-ending things with those videos. I shudder sometimes, and even wonder about footage that looks so professional, or when there are videos with people's phones clearly visible and obviously not doing the taping or recording.

I tell you these things only to caution you as a colleague. It is clear that no one starts out wanting to sully the reputation of a health professional. We are still seen by many as leaders in the community, an educated source of advice, and caring for the sick. I just think people are frustrated and disappointed when someone who mistreats patients repeatedly *seems not* to be cautioned by colleagues or peers who witness these things, and they appear to continue without reprimand or consequence. There is a boldness and arrogance often displayed by these providers because they do not believe they are touchable. They assume they are safe and the patient in front of them appears powerless. At the time, those patients are indeed vulnerable. But, as it turns out, it is not always a person without connections that we are treating. Their charts may say one thing, but they may be well connected! It is always unwise to judge a book by its cover.

I have a new friend who is a Sickle Cell advocate, but if you met him, you might be surprised. For one thing, he is Caucasian, blond, built and looks like a biker dude, with many tattoos. But his voice softens almost to tears as he talks about the suffering his wife with Sickle Cell endured before she passed, leaving a spirited daughter that he is raising. He is an ex-marine in the Hollywood entertainment business, and certainly has access to media and much more. He is well connected with the Sickle Cell community of 20,000 members online as he monitors his daughter, a star athlete. It is well known the deathly complications athletes can face playing professionally with just the Sickle Cell trait. So, he monitors her closely.

Due to of globalization, many more races are affected by Sickle Cell disease. It is not just Sub-Saharan Africa and the Mediterranean, the Arabian Peninsula, India, and Spanish speaking countries.[2] It is not unheard of to see someone with blond hair and light eyes with Sickle Cell disease. Furthermore, intermarriage has made it impossible to determine who is affected by Sickle Cell disease. It should be no surprise to hear that your Italian boss, who is married to a Spanish woman from Argentina, has a child with Sickle Cell disease.

References

1. "KKK membership sinks 2 Florida cops." MICHAEL WINTER USA TODAY July 14, 2014. https://amp.usatoday.com/amp/12645555
2. Your Guide to Understanding Sickle Cell Conditions" Genomics Home Reference, NIH, US National Library of Medicine, August 2012 https://ghr.nlm.nih.gov/condition/sickle-cell-disease#statistics

CHAPTER 16

THE TRICKLE DOWN EFFECT-RESEARCH AFFECTED

When patients are exposed repeatedly to a system they believe no longer cares for them, they stop trusting that system. Unfortunately, there are relatively innocent fields of medicine, like research and innovation, that might become "casualties of war." This is because while they were busy finding treatments and cures, and ways to improve on the management of Sickle Cell disease, some of their counterparts in healthcare were at times acting unprofessionally towards patients. This undoubtedly sours the pot for the Sickle Cell community and dampens the camaraderie these researchers are trying to establish with the patients. As a result, when they have completed their research, and lift their heads to come tell us their great findings, requesting our participation in further exploration, they find that they are not enthusiastically welcomed and wonder why. Enrolling patients for clinical research is more difficult than they would have anticipated, and they are met with some level distrust by the patients instead of an open willingness to help.

It confuses them further because they naturally think that our population, which has been left behind for so long in so many areas of medicine, would want to partner with them to correct the long-standing oversight. They do not process that they are part of the "Medical Establishment" that patients regard with a fair amount of disappointment and distrust for the wrongs that no one has apologized for. Furthermore, we are usually only made aware of the presence of research groups or pharmaceutical companies when they need something from us, but usually not before, and with no investment after.

This is the crux of the matter. When a person or organization does not apologize, it usually means one of two things;

- They have not realized the profound effect of the wounds they have caused, or

- They see it but, for whatever reason, lack humility to apologize.

These both have big implications. The first will take immense sensitivity training. But I believe the second one, while complex, may be more immediately fixable.

How? Just do it! Say something! Anything! Here is my recommendation based on just the hurts that I know exist in our circle as a result of our community experiencing the healthcare system.

First, it is important to say, "I see you!". We often feel ignored and invisible. Then say, "I want to hear what you have to say about having Sickle Cell disease. Maybe I can learn something". Say "I want you to know that I believe you and believe that your pain IS real." Lastly you say, "I am sorry that Sickle Cell management has been so substandard. As an organization, we were preoccupied and did not notice this, but we would love to work with you all directly to change things. Then ask, "how can I help?"

Asking a society how you can help and following up on that assistance is important. Some research and pharmaceutical industries have mistakenly tried to absolve themselves by just writing a check to an organization affiliated with our people. That is like insulting the people of a foreign country and then drafting a check to the government of that country, believing that suddenly the citizens would welcome you and do things for you. Obviously, it would be more fruitful to express your regrets directly to the citizens, and then schedule a visit in good faith.

It is certainly not wrong to contribute financially to organizations like The Sickle Cell Disease Association of America and Foundation for Sickle Cell Disease Research. They work tirelessly on behalf of a worldwide network of Sickle Cell patients, so of course, we need the help. But sometimes just "writing a check" without ever interacting with the people can make us wonder if our challenges with the medical establishment mean anything to you. It has the appearance of an entity that simply wants to write a check to make the atrocities disappear. There are many things we would gladly trade money for. We as a group would be moved with gratitude to see any influential body using their positions of power to help us remove some of our barriers to care.

So, come to us. Meet and talk with us, at home in our local groups and Sickle Cell conferences for patients and caregivers.

Don't just rent a booth and provide information on why we should come use your drug or enroll in trials. Let us see you and hear you and ask you questions and know that you are genuine in your desire to help us. If you are a friend, be there in times of crisis, and help. Be a continuous presence. As you invest in creating change and improving access to healthcare for us, we will see you as a supporter. This helps us let our collective guards down and work with you to participate in your drug trials, clinical trials, and medical surveys. I do believe there is hope in working together.

CHAPTER 17

FIRST DO NO HARM

History has treated us unkindly and left us without treatment for over a century. You are poised to be able to right some wrongs of that history. As such, I am asking you to please believe the patient in front of you the next time they present. Believe when they say the pain is still 10 out of 10, or that the drug stopped working two hours later. Find any and every means that you know how (I invite you to think outside of the box) and arrive at a treatment plan for that pain that is aggressive. Show the patient that you care. Invite them into a possible treatment plan that includes other things besides narcotic analgesics, but reassure them that you will not pull a medication that they may be depending on for pain management as you experiment with other things until you know that those experimental things work.

Push yourself to bend that arc of justice by arming yourself with any knowledge available for Sickle Cell disease guidance and management of acute pain. The 2014 expert guidelines have sat quietly and untouched for the most part, even by our pain management specialists and hematologists [1]. So many people are dying needlessly because of poor or grossly delayed care. Many providers don't even know that an acute vaso-occlusive

Sickle Cell crisis is supposed to be triaged as a level II according to the Emergency Severity Index, or ESI, the most prevalent 5-level emergency system in the United States.[2] This is a very high level, where patients should have been seen and evaluated by an emergency room physician and treatment started within one hour of their registration into the emergency department.

If this alone was implemented, we would save patients so much pain, ischemia to tissues, and end-organ damage, and decrease the financial burden on the healthcare system. I am asking you to do these things because the consequences for us patients are high. Every time that we experience more tissue death and end-organ damage, we become less qualified for clinical trials that are desiring excellent outcomes and so are choosing patients who do not have too many co-morbidities.

Being a part of a large Sickle Cell family of 20 thousand members allows me to see so many trends. I weep inside when I see recurring patterns of negative treatment, like patients being forced out of emergency rooms with greater than 7/10 pain because the laboratory results appeared normal. They are In Uganda, and Ghana, Zambia and all over Nigeria. And most definitely, they are all over these United States. They are reciting the same stories of mistreatment, so similar it's uncanny.

Because they hardly have the ear of their doctors, they will seek solace in each other, compare notes, and figure out what works and what doesn't long before the medical community gets clearance to clinically study their ailment. We are an n of 20,000, so trends become statistically significant.

Trust me, you will help more than you will be hustled by choosing to assist this community. Please remember that we patients are unfortunately veterans when it comes to opiate analgesics because of a lifetime of physical suffering, and so will not easily overdose. Providing that you are gauging for respiratory depression and blood pressure, you should be ok. Even these parameters are not quickly exceeded by a veteran patient, aside from other extenuating circumstances.

The opioid epidemic has made a lot of providers scared to treat. Others who have doubted our story of pain have used the restrictions initially imposed by the CDC [3]to withhold treatment, leaving us doubled over in pain as our internal organs become more compromised. And when the CDC stepped forward to clarify their stance and clearly exempted Sickle Cell from their restrictions on narcotic pain medication, many of these doctors did not change their practices. Please keep these exemptions by the CDC in mind so that you are unrestricted in treating us.[4]

And while you reflect on the CDC's exemption of restriction to treatment in Sickle Cell disease, please keep in mind the retrospective study done, which vindicated the Sickle Cell community. It was shown that while there was an exponential rise in opioid abuse and opioid-related deaths during the opioid epidemic, there was no correlative increase in the use of opioid in the Sickle Cell population.[5] There was no increase in deaths from opioid drug overdose in the Sickle Cell population.[5] This screams of exoneration for all the negative press Sickle Cell patients receive about the number of medications used to palliate their pain. It also points out that most of our fears as providers in treating patients having

Sickle Cell disease with large doses of narcotic analgesics are grossly unfounded.

We need our providers to stop the pain related stress response that starts to happen with the onset of an acute episode of pain in the Sickle Cell crisis. Right now, it seems that the best you have is narcotic analgesic medications. At least that is what you have told us so far. If you had told us the best thing you had for stopping our pain was steroids, we would have taken them, even with their side effects.

I know because when it became apparent that my adrenals were stressed and not producing sufficiently to cover me, and this was also worsening my Sickle Cell pain, I gladly asked for steroids to be added to my regimen. When I experienced significant relief in my pain, I was elated. Prior to this, I was afraid of dropping out of my Family Practice residency because I had almost daily recurring pain. It was likely from the stress of residency. When we finally figured out that I actually needed the steroids on a long-term basis, I was petrified of the potential long-term damage from the steroids. But I was even more petrified at the thought of living daily with the level of pain I was then experiencing.

So yes, with the help of my hematologist who presented my case to "grand rounds" (meeting of many doctors of the same specialty to create an ad hoc expert panel and discuss difficult cases), I was placed on steroids. Later, I sought out an endocrinologist and was tapered only to physiologic doses for safety reasons. It only covered my pain partially, and I was sad because I had been hoping to finally ditch any therapy I received from those opiates by covering with the steroids. However, I was talked out of that option and encouraged to go with lifelong therapy of opiates instead because the side effect profile of long-term steroids use with Sickle Cell was much worse.

I am not the only one who would take another treatment if it worked. This has been the frustration of the Sickle Cell community. If you can think of something else, we will gladly take it. Until then, use what you have and cover us well. Our organs are depending on it. We would like to stay intact and live as long as possible.

References

1. Evidence Based Management of Sickle Cell Disease Expert Panel 2014 https://www.nhlbi.nih.gov/sites/default/files/media/docs/sickle-cell-disease
2. "Managing Acute Complications of Sickle Cell Disease," Evidence Based Management of Sickle Cell Disease Expert Panel 2014, Chapter3, p31-32 https://www.nhlbi.nih.gov/sites/default/files/media/docs/sickle-cell-disease
3. "Opioid crisis adds to pain of Sickle Cell patients" NIH, NHLBI September 15, 2017 https://www.nhlbi.nih.gov/news/2017/opioid-crisis-adds-pain-sickle-cell-patients
4. CDC Clarifies Guideline on Opioid Prescribing for Chronic Pain Physician's Weekly, Apr 12, 2019 https://www.physiciansweekly.com/cdc-clarifies-guideline-on-opioid-prescribing-for-chronic-pain/
5. "Hospitals See No Link Between US Opioid Crisis and Patients' Use of Treatment, Study Reports" Sickle Cell Anemia News, Jose Marques PHD, JANUARY 3, 2019 https://sicklecellanemianews.com/2019/01/03/opioid-abuse-not-seen-in-in-hospital-death-rates/

CHAPTER 18

We CAN DO This!

In the Sickle Cell community, we refer to ourselves as Sickle Cell warriors. This term has a wonderful history of how it was coined by a nurse who was searching for an online support community for Sickle Cell disease but found none, even in 2005. The community quickly came to identify with the description. Truthfully, with every crisis, we fight for our lives, and it feels like another battle. Your body screams, "you are not coming out of this one," and then somehow, you do. Often, you have battle wounds and scars to show for your ordeal. So "warriors," I believe, is a very appropriate designation to this community of people who suffer indescribably severe pain and still get up, go out and live the day after.

But if we are warriors fighting a war, we need a battle plan— a good one! Right now, we are getting killed because there is no clear plan for victory. Things change from one treatment center to the next and drastically, too. We are always on the defensive. We need to be on the offensive. We need a "plan of attack."

There is much that we need to do as a community, and I will address this in another space. But our providers have a part as well. The first part is to admit that you need help. This is a big step. Admission is half the battle because then you allow yourselves to be teachable. Truly all we want is a partnership in our care, where, if we have some information and pass it along to you, you will not feel upstaged but helped. And trust me, when people feel like you have partnered with them in their care, and you are listening to them, if something goes wrong, the blame will likely be shared. No one wants to come after a provider they feel is fighting for them. So, let's hold hands and tackle this thing together, shall we?

TREATMENT PLAN:

The first thing I want to do is find a protocol that works and model our Sickle Cell protocol after that one. Why reinvent the wheel, right? The one that comes to mind is the protocol for Acute Coronary Syndrome, or ACS, of which heart attack is a subset.

When I was doing my residency, there was a mnemonic for immediate treatment of ACS upon presentation called MONAB- morphine, oxygen, nitrate, aspirin, beta blocker.[1]

This was the basics. This was the starting point. And this was for everyone who walked in with high-probability ACS. They were seen immediately, and treatment started to prevent any worsening ischemia to the heart muscle. Prevent ischemia! Sounds familiar?

We can borrow a few things from this protocol, including the urgency of application and the plan to prevent worsening ischemia. This is for protocol.

The next component of the battle plan is dealing with cultural sensitivity when it comes to pain management in Sickle Cell disease. For help with this, we can study the general treatment of cancer patients.

In general, we are very gentle with cancer patients. We realize that they are fighting a difficult and physically painful battle, and the last thing we want to do is add to that pain. Can you imagine leaving a cancer patient sitting in the waiting room of the Emergency Department crying in pain? No! How do we know that they are really in pain? We don't, but we figure why else they would be there, right? Besides, cancer is known to be painful at certain stages. Even if we don't know what stage their cancer is, we give them the benefit of doubt.

Now let's use that for Sickle Cell disease, a disease that can be easily confirmed with a blood test. Furthermore, many patients have a mediport or port-a-cath, usually indicating that our disease is active, and we have had to undergo a surgical procedure to implant this device for better venous access. The literature confirms the severity of pain in Sickle Cell, so this is not a subject of debate. Realize we are fighting a hard battle, and the last thing you want to do is add to that pain. And we do have severe pain when we present for treatment - why else would we be there?

For each person presenting to the emergency room in a Sickle Cell crisis, the assumption should be that there is a vaso-occlusive crisis (or VOC, meaning blockage of vessels by sickling, causing ischemia) [2]. However, a work-up should be done quickly to rule out any other inciting agents, like a bacterial infection (high degree of suspicion with this disorder). It is important to note that this work-up should only be happening *after* the patient has been started on treatment for pain control because until you stop the stress response that the pain is causing, the patient's tissues are still being damaged, and they are experiencing worsening ischemia. Pain management, in this case, is not for comfort, but a means of lessening the damage.

For some guidance on the practical application of this, we should embrace the NIH 2014 Guidelines (expected to be updated by the end of 2019), "Evidence-Based Management of Sickle Cell Disease" [3] and focus our attention on chapter three, "Managing Acute Complications of Sickle Cell Disease." Here is an excerpt:

"Pain management must be guided by the patient report of pain severity. No biomarkers or imaging studies can validate pain or assess its severity. The primary management of a VOC is analgesic treatment, typically with opioids. No empirical data exist to indicate that rapid analgesic administration results in better outcomes. However, as patients with VOC present with severe pain and are at risk for other complications, best practice suggests that rapid triage, placement, and administration of analgesics should be encouraged. The Emergency Severity Index (ESI) Version 4 triage system, which is used by more than half of emergency departments in the United States, suggests that persons with SCD be triaged as ESI level 2, a very high priority, and rapid placement be facilitated."[2]

If this subjective measure of treatment of pain gives you cause for pause, please may I remind you that as long as this diagnosis is legitimate for the patient you are treating, you should practice not worrying about administering pain management. You are not expected to guess how much pain someone is in, but only to check that they have a diagnosis that warrants that pain. So, we are all set here.

The next concern is usually what to give for pain. Again, just like everyone with cancer pain will respond differently, and we rely on those patients to tell us what has worked, we will do the same here. Regardless of which medication is being taken for pain at home, the guidelines are the same on how to manage that patient, taking their individual regimen into account.

"A recommendation is included to guide providers in managing persons who take both long- and short-acting opioids to manage pain at home. There are no empirical data to guide whether or not to continue long-acting opioids when ordering continuous opioids via patient-controlled analgesia (PCA). The decision to continue long-acting oral opioids should be made on an individual basis. In most circumstances, it is advisable to continue oral long-acting opioids, including methadone therapy, even when ordering continuous opioids via PCA to ensure adequate pain relief while avoiding a break in coverage and preventing withdrawal." [3]

The Guidelines are also quite helpful in providing algorithms for navigating your way throughout pain management, giving intervals for redosing a medication and the management of the patient in an inpatient setting. Furthermore, there are recommendations for treatments of each body system in an acute or chronic presentation, so keeping these guidelines close is highly advisable.

Because they know that you are busy professionals, the American Society of Hematology has sifted the NIH 2014 guidelines and condensed the vital information from them into pocket guides for both acute and chronic management of Sickle Cell. They are available as free downloads.[4] It couldn't get any easier than that for access.

There are many other valuable resources that I could share with you. However, my goal is not to impress you with the number of resources I can find. My goal is to provide you with a few vital guidelines and ask that you kindly enforce them. I think as a community, we would much prefer that.

A PLAN OF SUPPORT

The second part of the battle plan is making sure that the patient has a support network. There was a time in the late 1990's when I was sent, as a patient, to attend the support groups of the Leukemia society meeting at the hospital where I was being treated, because no one knew of any support groups for Sickle Cell disease. When I eventually found a Yahoo email group of patients and caregivers dealing with Sickle Cell, I was elated.

In one session of talking with the members, I learned that I was triggering crises after cross country flights to see my family because my system, like some with Sickle Cell, was getting stressed with altitude. I needed supplemental oxygen when flying.

Meanwhile, my doctors insisted that since it was a pressurized air cabin, I should be fine. Once I started purchasing the overhead oxygen with my flights, my crises stopped. I could go home to visit my family each holiday without fear of heading to the emergency room upon landing.

My point is that we need support groups because some things that are happening to us are not yet in the textbooks. Especially for a disease that has not yet been fully studied, I have found that many times, just the sheer volume of patients in these support groups allows us to compare notes and see trends. As patients, we can be a great resource for each other in a way you as a provider may never be able to be for your patients. Take part of the patient's visit to talk about support groups, and make sure that they are plugged into a supportive community.

Patients may not know that this support exists. You could suggest these networks of support to your patients, and I will make a list of some that are available *and* informative.[5] You would improve their lives, both emotionally and physically, just with this tiny step. I also moderate an online support group where I teach about 1200 members as much as possible on subjects relevant to us. It is comparatively a much smaller group, so I'm still able to answers questions posed by group members. I want every Sickle Cell warrior to be a "thriver and not just a survivor." This link will also be in the back of the book. [5]

The topic of seeing a counselor should always come up. Living with this disease can be a humbling and often lonely experience. The emotional pain is further exacerbated by the insensitivity we experience from the healthcare system as we access treatment for our disease. We can begin to feel marginalized and insignificant. The ability to talk through these feelings is crucial as it affects how we interact with people and critical life decisions we make.

It is often not just the patient that needs support, but the doctor too! This is where I believe that Project ECHO that I spoke about in chapter one can be helpful. This project, if conducted well, has the potential to help providers, by establishing a peer relationship where ideas can be exchanged. It appears that the available hubs (expert panels in operation) have nicely broken up the country's map to ensure all states are covered by at least one of the hubs. I will include the link that provides this information and a list of the contact person for each region. [6]

The only other thing that I would suggest would be a support for both the patient and the doctor, depending on which doctor you are. Here is my thought. At one point, my care became problematic as an inpatient because I would present with vaso-occlusive crises that were awful and required a high dose of narcotic analgesic. To make matters worse, because I did not fully understand the time-sensitive nature of things, I would wait until I was practically hallucinating in pain before turning myself in to the emergency room because I was always afraid of experiencing new doctors each time who didn't know me. This often made it difficult for them to break my pain because it had gotten quite a head start.

Once my hematologist Dr. Beth became aware of why I stayed away from the emergency room, she spoke with me about my desired pain medication regimen as an inpatient, in terms of what really helped to break my pain. She then dictated a letter into my medical records in the electronic system of the hospital. The letter essentially vouched for me, saying that I was someone who did not utilize medication unless I had to, so if I presented to the E.D, just admit me and rule out infection but first make sure to address my pain in the following way. She described the regimen we spoke about in the letter and dictated a number where she could be reached by a physician (I agreed never to call it directly.) Then I was given a copy of that letter, as well as my husband and "adopted" parents. That one thing changed the way I experienced the emergency room for the better.

I believe that the hematologists have this same ability to improve the experience a patient receives.

Ideally, we should have a separate center that could treat acute uncomplicated VOCs with the required medication. However, until there exists something like this, where the staff is permanent, and we can reduce the anxiety around first time meetings with providers we hope will like us and treat us well, a letter would help greatly. It also helps the emergency provider to get a letter from someone who knows us well (trust) and can speak to our pain.

The nurses could use some support too!

In an inpatient setting, one of my hospitals was known to lower the ratio of patients to nurses in the oncology ward because of the complexity of oncology patients. I believe that if the Guidelines are enforced where we patients are attended to quickly with pain management to minimize end-organ damage, the nurses will benefit from classifying us as an oncology patient for the purpose of decreasing the ratio. After all, we are seen by the Hematology/Oncology department for outpatient care. The other option is to simply decrease the ratio regardless of which floor we are admitted to.

The feedback from nurses is that when they are busy and get another high maintenance patient, this can often cause a frustration that could be transferred to the patient. It is not good to have these negative feelings of frustration persist and always associated with us when we are admitted. This will not help with cultural sensitivity issues. On the other hand, the nurse looks forward to a patient like us when she is given the proper allotment of time for our care. But more than this, the improvement in response time to manage our pain and prevent end-organ damage will reduce our hospital stay as pain is controlled quicker, and we return to baseline sooner.

BREAK OUT THE RESOURCES

Lastly, there should be resources that provide a little more hope and help than pain control. These include all the medications that will soon be available for the management of Sickle Cell disease. As I said in Chapter one, these are indeed exciting times for Sickle Cell disease. Every provider treating Sickle Cell patients should know the treatments available and how to connect with any information available for these treatments. Endari is already on the market, and Voxelotor and Crizanlizumab are supposed to be available starting early 2020.

Know about the clinical trials in case we would like to participate. Someone in the office can quickly check on clinicaltrials.gov for information, but a call to the NIH does not hurt either. And chances are, if you have done well in getting your patient connected with online support groups, they will know what's coming down the pipeline, what clinical trials they would like to enroll in or what medications they may want to try.

ALL RISE!

I believe all providers would like to see a day when Sickle Cell patients do not have to rely solely on narcotic analgesics for therapy, especially knowing that it does not address the damage occurring in our bodies. Your desire to seek a true treatment for us should be propelled by your conviction to see us minimize or even eliminate the use of pain medications.

If I may be so bold as to suggest some preventive medicine here, we should also be referred to a nutritionist or at least be given the offer to see one. Some of our circulation problems appear to me to be very similar to those of a diabetic, who are usually referred for diet and education. Furthermore, many of us may be at risk with our glucose levels. Hemoglobin A-1 C is a standard measurement for risk of diabetes, but with Sickle Cell, our red blood cells (with our hemoglobin) die and are recycled every 30 days, not every three months as is the customary testing. We would likely have a great hemoglobin A-1 C results, even when our sugars are not controlled.

Sugar is dangerous to the Sickle Cell patient, just as it is to the diabetic patient. Inflammation and scarring of the vessels are imminent. And before you know it, circulation is compromised, and tissue damage inevitable from ischemia.

So why does this matter? It matters because our understanding of Sickle Cell disease physiology is so behind that we would order a normal diet on a patient in terrible crisis and allow for packets upon packets of cookies and cakes, juices and sodas to be fed to the patient while in the throes of their disease. We patients are in desperate need of education and certainly can benefit from how to eat for the management of our Sickle Cell disease.

Reference

1. Morphine, Oxygen, Nitrates, and Mortality Reducing Pharmacological Treatment for Acute Coronary Syndrome: An Evidence-based Review José Nunes de Alencar Neto Cureus. 2018 Jan 25; 10(1): e2114. https://www.ncbi.nlm.nih.gov/pmc/articles/PMC5866121/

2. "Managing Acute Complications of Sickle Cell Disease" ,Evidence Based Management of Sickle Cell Disease Expert Panel 2014, Chapter 3, p31 https://www.nhlbi.nih.gov/sites/default/files/media/docs/sickle-cell-disease

3. "Managing Acute Complications of Sickle Cell Disease" ,Evidence Based Management of Sickle Cell Disease Expert Panel 2014, Chapter3, p31-36 https://www.nhlbi.nih.gov/sites/default/files/media/docs/sickle-cell-disease

4. "Management of Acute Complications of Sickle Cell Disease ; A Pocket Guide for the Clinician" by Timothy McCavit MD,MSCS and Payal Desai MD https://www.hematology.org/Clinicians/Guidelines-Quality/Quick-Ref/3466.aspx

5. List of Available and informative Facebook Sickle Cell Support Groups:

   a) Bedtime Stories with Dr. Simone-Sickle Cell Thriver (my group) https://www.facebook.com/groups/504007816766590/

   b) Sickle Cell Warriors Unity https://www.facebook.com/groups/300152443524848/

   c) Sickle Cell 101 https://www.facebook.com/SickleCell101/

   d) Sickle Cell Anemia & Sickle Cell Trait God Bless Group https://www.facebook.com/groups/227940910712991/

6. https://www.nichq.org/sites/default/files/inline-files/
   Project_ECHO_FINAL.pdf

Northeast Region: Sickle Cell Disease TeleECHO Clinic hosted by Johns Hopkins University (DC, MD, NJ, NY, VA, PA, DE, WV, Virgin Islands, Puerto Rico) bailey.house@jhu.edu

Midwest Region: STORM TeleECHO (IL, IN, MI, MN, OH, WI) storm@cchmc.org

Pacific Region: Western States Telementoring Collaborative for Sickle Cell Disease (AK, AZ, CA, ID, HI, OR, NV, WA) jennkim@mail.cho.org

7. Hemoglobin A1c Test (HbA1c) Melissa Conrad Stöppler, MD, William C. Shiel Jr., MD, FACP, FACR eMedicinehealth *6/17/2019* https://www.emedicinehealth.com/hemoglobin_a1c_hba1c/article_em.htm

CONCLUSION

If you have taken the time to read this book, I want to say a heartfelt thank you! It means you care for this community or at least someone who exists in it.

In the very near future, you will have so many more treatments at your disposal. Use them wisely. There may even be information that can help patients with Sickle Cell apply for gene therapy-a cure to offer! Know this information! Don't let it just exist out there in the cosmos! Show your patients where to go. Don't leave them to fend for themselves in their vulnerable state. Don't put their bodies at risk of further end-organ damage that might disqualify them for a cure, simply because you did not care enough. Don't let that be on your conscience. Do something.

And when we present in a Sickle Cell Pain crisis to the emergency room, don't assume we are drug-seeking because we have not yet accessed one of these treatments. Assume the best. I have reacted to hydroxyurea to the point that my fingernails and toenails were dark grey in color. The palms of my hands and the soles of my feet were black as though I had played in a coal mine. I so wanted to be better that I held on to the treatment even as this happened to me for two years. Yet, when I was asked about why I was not on hydroxyurea, I felt a judgment that I somehow had not tried hard enough. If someone tried something and says it did not work for them, let that be.

This scenario will likely happen for other patients as the other treatments come into existence. Some of us are scared of what we consider "genetic tinkering," or the potential side effects of all the treatments coming down the pipeline. Give us time to grow, help inform us, and remind us that you do not have all the answers. This would be a good point to encourage us to ask around in our support groups about what the experience has been for any given treatment.

We are many, we do many things, and we live the best life we can with incredible pain. I have often said that if I did not feel this pain myself, I probably would never believe that someone could feel that level of pain and be alive. I would think people were faking it! So, I understand! Maybe that is why this disease was given to me, to be able to address the medical community and help to represent-and vindicate- the Sickle Cell community. It is also to explain the things we as patients are experiencing in a way that the medical community could begin to understand.

I am hoping that I can continue my work of bridging the gap a little more between the two communities by addressing my own community. I have tried to shed light on some unique challenges we face in the medical community. In the future, I hope to further the dialogue by highlighting the companies, organizations and especially the individuals (hopefully this includes you) that may want to extend that olive branch and work with us. I hope that this day comes soon.

Made in the USA
Las Vegas, NV
14 March 2021